Policies for small enterprises

Creating
the right environment
for good jobs

Policies for small enterprises

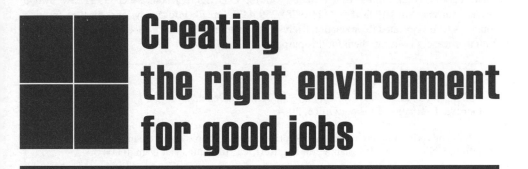

Creating the right environment for good jobs

Gerhard Reinecke and Simon White

 INTERNATIONAL LABOUR OFFICE • GENEVA

Reinecke, G.; White, S.
Policies for small enterprises: Creating the right environment for good jobs
Geneva, International Labour Office, 2004

Small enterprise, micro-enterprise, enterprise creation, employment creation, government policy, Chile, Guinea, Pakistan, Peru, South Africa, Tanzania, Viet Nam. 03.04.5

ISBN 92-2-113724-4

ILO Cataloguing in Publication Data

Typeset by Magheross Graphics, France & Ireland *www.magheross.com*
Printed and bound in Great Britain by Biddles Ltd, Kings Lynn, Norfolk

CONTENTS

TABLES

FIGURES

ACKNOWLEDGEMENTS

This book is the result of a collective effort as part of the policy research and reform programme of the ILO's InFocus Programme on boosting employment through Small EnterprisE Development (ILO/SEED). It synthesizes some of the main results of a seven-country research project to analyse the link between the policy environment for micro- and small enterprises and the quantity and quality of employment created by these enterprises. The book draws from a range of papers commissioned for this research project. Although they are not always cited, these papers are the main empirical basis for this book, which could not have been drafted without them. The list on page xxi provides the full references.

The following national consultants conducted the research in the selected countries: Carolina Flores (Chile), Moussa Kourouma (Guinea), Atif Salim Malik from the Small and Medium Enterprise Development Authority (Pakistan), Juan Chacaltana from the Centro de Estudios para el Desarrollo y la Participación (Peru), Jennifer Mollentz from the Community Agency for Social Enquiry (South Africa), Paula Tibandebage from the Economic and Social Research Foundation (United Republic of Tanzania), and Pham Thi Thu Hang from the Viet Nam Chamber of Commerce and Industry (Viet Nam).

Surveys of micro- and small enterprises were coordinated by the following researchers: Malva Espinosa (Chile), Moussa Kourouma (Guinea), Ijaz Gilani from Gallup (Pakistan), Meybol Gómez from the Ministerio de Trabajo y Promoción Social (Peru), Patrick Burton from DRA (South Africa),

Marcellina Chijoriga from the University of Dar es Salaam (United Republic of Tanzania), and Pham Thi Thu Hang from the Viet Nam Chamber of Commerce and Industry. Micheline Goedhuys provided a major contribution to the analysis of the survey results across the seven countries.

The authors wish to acknowledge the following people who participated in this research project. In ILO/SEED, Christine Evans-Klock, Christine Enzler and Jens Dyring Christensen were part of the research team and provided a significant contribution to the design of this research along with technical assistance in the assessment of its findings as well as in supporting and monitoring national consultants.

Other colleagues in ILO/SEED contributed with suggestions on how to incorporate the dimensions of gender, job quality and effective implementation into the research design and research tools, as well as with comments on earlier drafts. These include Gavin Anderson, Martin Clemensson, Gerry Finnegan, Roel Hakemulder, Andrea Singh, Jim Tanburn and Rie Vejs-Kjeldgaard.

In other ILO units as well, several colleagues took the time to read earlier drafts and make detailed comments, including Peter Auer, Duncan Campbell, Wouter van Ginneken, Jane Hodges and Terje Tessem. Craig Churchill, Dominique Gross and Peter van Rooij gave inputs in briefing national consultants and commented on research results on finance policy. Several reviewers, both inside and outside the ILO, helped us to improve the text. Thanks are also due to the Bureau of Publications, and especially to Charlotte Beauchamp for excellent editing.

This research benefited from the logistical support and technical feedback from a number of colleagues in ILO field offices, including Jacobo Varela, Mario Tueros, Max Iacono, Gopal Joshi, Samina Rauf Hasan, Flora Minja, André Bogui and Bassirou Tidjani. We wish to thank them for their important contribution.

It goes without saying that the authors are responsible for remaining errors and shortcomings.

Santiago de Chile
Perth, Australia
August 2003

EXECUTIVE SUMMARY

About this book

Around the world, governments are coming to realize the important roles micro- and small enterprises (MSEs) can play in social and economic development. Not only do MSEs create employment for a vast majority of women and men, they also undertake productive activities that contribute to the national accounts and reduce poverty. Small in size at the firm level, the broader MSE sector can be a major engine for national development.

Although most governments have recognized the potential of MSEs to create employment and contribute to poverty eradication, in many cases this potential is not being fulfilled. Many workers in MSEs face poor working conditions and incomes that are too low to leave poverty behind. The policy and regulatory environment in which these MSEs work is determined by government, yet this environment is often part of the problem rather than part of the solution. Reforms are badly needed to provide a level playing field.

This book shows how policies and laws established by the State can contribute to the creation of more and better jobs for women and men in MSEs. It can help policy-makers, development practitioners and researchers to reform the policy and legal environment so that it becomes more conducive to the growth of MSEs and the quality and number of jobs they create.

Original research in seven developing countries

The research on which this book is based has been commissioned and supported by the ILO and carried out by national consultants and research institutions in seven developing countries: Chile, Guinea, Pakistan, Peru, South Africa, the United Republic of Tanzania and Viet Nam. Each country study included careful mapping and analysis of policies and laws, an analysis of employment and establishment data, stakeholder interviews and workshops, and a survey of approximately 300 MSEs to analyse their response to the policy and legal environment. Several common problems have been uncovered by this research, as well as instances illustrating good practice. Thus, while not providing simple recipes for success, the findings presented here have potential for broad application.

Using the enterprise-level data gathered in these seven countries, new light is shed on the impact of policies on enterprise conduct and performance. The book analyses employment dynamics in MSEs in the seven countries and relates successful employment growth and investment behaviour to the underlying policy differences across countries.

The two sides of MSE employment

MSEs provide most employment ...

Micro- and small enterprises have become regarded as a vital element in modern, dynamic economies. Policy-makers and economists value their flexibility and ability to adapt and to find niche markets as employment patterns and economic systems shift away from the dominance of large or public enterprises. In all seven countries under study, employment in MSEs accounts for the majority of non-agricultural employment, and in six of them, their share has been increasing over the 1990s.

Does this mean that MSEs have provided a solution to the employment challenge and helped to combat poverty? Unfortunately, in many cases, new jobs in MSEs simply replace jobs lost elsewhere – due to the downsizing of large enterprises or of the public sector, for example. Data from Chile and Peru show that statistically, a growing share of MSEs in employment is correlated with economic downturns rather than periods of fast economic growth. Moreover, many jobs in MSEs are of poor quality: incomes may be at poverty level; dangerous working conditions can put workers at risk of losing their livelihood through work-related illness or accident; and few MSEs are covered by the social security systems that protect workers against such risks.

Many MSEs in the seven countries under study are survivalist in nature, rather than responding to market opportunities. Women, in particular, are often required to undertake some kind of income-generating or enterprise activity to supplement insufficient household incomes. There are tremendous differences between the most fragile and precarious micro-enterprises and the most dynamic and prosperous small enterprises. Clearly, a growing employment share of MSEs is not a goal in itself: everything depends on the type of enterprises, their likelihood of graduating from micro- to small or medium-sized enterprises, and the job quality for their owners and workers. MSEs can have a crucial role in development, but they are not a panacea that automatically solves the pressing problems of unemployment, underemployment and poverty.

... but are not a panacea for overcoming poverty

This does not mean that development efforts should focus on large enterprises and neglect smaller ones. Development strategies focused on large enterprises were applied during the 1970s and 1980s and mostly failed to provide employment opportunities beyond the enterprises directly favoured by these policy measures.

Because of the huge number of persons employed in MSEs, changes to the policy and legal environment that create even small improvements by increasing incomes and job quality can make an important contribution to collective welfare. While salaried workers in MSEs earn less on average than salaried workers in larger enterprises, becoming self-employed can be a viable alternative for many low-income workers. In addition, the majority of MSE owner-managers themselves value the independence and income-generating opportunities provided by running a business, despite difficult conditions. Only in South Africa and the United Republic of Tanzania did a high share of surveyed MSE owner-managers indicate that the main reason for them being in business was the termination of previous employment or the lack of other job opportunities.

Why policies and laws make a difference for MSEs

MSEs are often thought of as operating independently of laws and regulations – especially those operating in the informal economy. Indeed, many MSE owner-managers choose not to comply with regulations and, according to our MSE surveys, most see markets as the main factor influencing their operations and employment decisions.

MSEs are not outside the scope of policies and laws

However, this does not mean that policies and laws are not important. Simply, their impact is often invisible or indirect. For example, an MSE that hides from government authorities to avoid registration is affected by regulations precisely because the attempt to evade them prevents the enterprise from becoming more visible, using more publicity, or expanding.

When many MSE owner-managers choose not to comply with the policies and laws of the State, they remain hidden, either by keeping their employment levels below specified thresholds (for example, in Pakistan, MSEs with a workforce below ten are not required to comply with several labour laws) or by operating informally. This creates a situation in which workers in the MSE sector can be poorly paid, insecure and placed in harmful situations. As a consequence, MSEs can be marginalized in a low-cost/low-productivity trap.

Compliance with regulations has costs for MSEs but can bring important benefits

Most MSEs are neither completely formal nor completely informal: they comply with some regulations while evading others. Compliance with regulations is thus a continuum. A higher degree of compliance has benefits for both the enterprise and its workers. For example, our research found that those MSEs that complied with basic registration requirements had better access to financial services and provided better social security coverage to their workers. Enterprises that complied with registration requirements were found to create more employment over time than MSEs that did not comply, even after accounting for differences in initial size, enterprise age and economic sector. Policies and laws that are biased against MSEs can reduce the rate of compliance and, hence, reduce employment in MSEs.

On the other hand, facilitating compliance can boost the quantity and quality of jobs. In Viet Nam, the new Enterprise Law has made registration easier; while around 5,000 enterprises per year were registered under the previous law, this figure has jumped up to around 15,000 per year since then. About 70 per cent of these enterprises are truly new, while the remainder is accounted for by the regularization of previously unregistered enterprises.

Compliance with laws and regulations always comes at a cost, but it also opens up opportunities for growth. Reducing the costs of compliance while increasing the benefits makes a crucial difference for MSEs in their efforts to generate a livelihood for their owners and workers.

Help or hindrance? Government's role in MSE employment

In most countries, the government's approach to MSEs is contradictory. On the one hand, government-sponsored projects and programmes are designed and implemented to provide support to MSEs. On the other hand, however, the broader environment of policies, laws and regulations is biased against MSEs, compared to larger enterprises. This paradox was the main motivation for us to look at the policy and legal environment in six main policy fields, rather than only assessing MSE support policies.

A conventional approach taken by many governments has been to provide financial and business development services to MSEs, either directly through their own agencies, or through intermediary agencies that may be closer to the target group and more market-oriented. However, they have often fallen short in their delivery. This is mainly for two reasons: first, because government programmes are finite and can only reach a limited number of enterprises; second, because there are broader influences affecting the business environment in which MSEs operate, which can undermine the impact of specific government programmes.

From support programmes to a conducive environment

While MSE support programmes only reach a small proportion of enterprises in a country, anti-MSE biases in the policy and legal environment hinder the development of the majority of MSEs in a country. MSEs are often faced with costs of compliance that are proportionally greater than those incurred by medium-sized and large enterprises. While such biases are not always intended, fully understood, or even immediately visible, they can significantly affect the behaviour of MSE owner-managers.

By removing unnecessary policy and legal constraints to MSE activity, governments can enhance the capacity of the MSE sector to contribute to national social and economic goals. However, deregulation is not the only answer to unleashing the potential of small enterprises. Regulations are necessary, for instance to protect workers from exploitative practices, or consumers from health hazards. On the other hand, government policies can open up market opportunities, for example by re-designing public tendering procedures in view of MSE participation or by ensuring MSEs' access to export incentive schemes.

The challenge of policy implementation

Policies are often designed without a clear strategy of implementation. In many cases, communication of policies and laws to the MSE sector is insufficient. In Pakistan, for example, information on many laws and regulations is provided in English despite the fact that the majority of the population understands and reads Urdu only. In addition, the lack of transparency and the insufficient coordination between various government agencies hinder the effective implementation of policies and laws.

This study provides a strong argument for national governments to adopt a developmental approach to the MSE sector. Such an approach removes any anti-MSE biases in the policy and legal environment, while promoting MSE growth by facilitating compliance with policies and laws designed to maximize the role and contribution of MSEs in national development.

Common problems and examples of good practice

The review of six policy areas that are particularly relevant to the operations of MSEs distinguishes a number of common problems in the policy and legal environment while also finding examples of good practice. In each of these fields, the dangers of an anti-MSE bias have been identified, as well as instances where governments have adopted innovative or developmental approaches. If adequately adapted to national circumstances, this analysis may provide elements for policy reform beyond the countries studied.

Analysing different policy areas

Specific small enterprise promotion policies already exist in four out of the seven countries under study, while they are under discussion in Guinea and the United Republic of Tanzania. Although these policies do not create more conducive policy environments by themselves, they can be a tool in the process of improving policies and laws and establishing mechanisms to provide services to MSEs. For example, in South Africa, the National Small Business Act (1996) encourages government departments to assess the impact of policies and laws on small enterprises, and a detailed impact assessment study was carried out before deciding on the application of the Basic Conditions of Employment Act (1997) to MSEs.

Complying with **business laws and regulations** is a higher burden on MSEs than on larger enterprises. In many cases, not even government officials know the relevant laws and regulations to establish and run a small enterprise. Moreover, many laws and regulations do not seem to have a clearly defined purpose. In trying to comply with these complex regulations, MSE owner-managers have to spend time and energy that could be better invested in complying with labour law and improving job quality. To improve the situation, business laws and regulations should be reviewed to identify any requirements that do not serve any purpose. Overlaps and contradictions between registration requirements with different agencies should be eliminated. Reporting requirements can be harmonized across government agencies (intervals and formats). In some cases, licences may be replaced with simple registration requirements without discretionary power for government officials.

In many countries, **labour policies** are not tailored to MSEs' needs. Many MSEs are constrained by the high cost of compliance and workers are left unprotected. While governments need to be realistic as to the capacity of MSEs to comply with labour regulations, there should be no general exemptions from basic labour norms given to MSEs. Instead, overly complex regulations should be streamlined, specific norms should be simplified based on careful assessment of the capacity of MSEs to comply with them, and mechanisms of implementation should be improved beyond labour inspections alone. These are better means to meet the twin objectives of employment creation and job quality. For example, Chile has placed emphasis on flexible laws that combine fines with training in legal standards for MSEs.

Although MSEs are often thought to be outside the scope of **taxation**, this idea does not correspond to reality because most MSEs do pay taxes in one form or another. In fact, tax regulations are the regulations that are most strongly enforced on MSEs. In all countries under study except South Africa, over 80 per cent of small urban enterprises in the MSE survey sample were registered for business income tax purposes. Given the fragility of many MSEs, they are strongly affected by the complexities of most tax systems and the risk of being harassed by tax officials. Some countries have already succeeded in simplifying their tax systems. For example, Peru has concentrated the tax administration in one single tax authority, introduced simple procedures for compliance and established two special tax regimes to facilitate the entry of micro-enterprises into the system.

In the field of **trade policies**, the policies that have been designed to facilitate enterprises' export orientation often exclude MSEs through minimum transaction volumes or cumbersome administrative procedures. Thus, while many MSEs participate in international trade as providers for export enterprises, they seldom benefit from the incentives that go to direct exporters. This anti-MSE bias lessens the potential benefits of the trade liberalization policies applied during the 1990s, which in principle diminished the anti-MSEs bias inherent in the import-substitution strategies of the 1970s and 1980s.

Finance policies are a key factor to improving MSEs' capacity to create more and better jobs. While projects and programmes are abundant, these often have limited outreach. Sound finance policies can give MSEs better access to finance by reducing risks and transaction costs for financial institutions. In all countries, compliance with laws and regulations in other policy fields, such as business registration, taxation and labour, helped MSEs obtain credit from formal credit providers. Among the countries under study, Chile has been quite successful in incorporating MSEs into the banking system. This success was due to a series of factors, including a credit line for micro-enterprises that is managed by the main public finance institution; credit lines for MSEs tendered by the State and administered by commercial banks; and the advanced development of financial regulations and the banking system. Most private banks are now reaching out to MSEs as potential customers.

While the lessons from the analysis of the six policy areas are important for policy reform, each country has to find its own solutions. Several elements are central for successful reform: assessing the current policies and regulations before changing them; hearing the voice of MSEs and other stakeholders; and recognizing gender biases, whether these are due to the policies and laws affecting MSEs or rooted in the broader legal and economic context. When reforming the policy and legal environment it can be useful to have examples of good practice in other countries. We hope that this book provides a resource for policy-makers and advocates who are engaged in these processes. Our study has clearly shown that review and reform is a continuous process. This book can guide the review and reform of policy and legal environments to tap the potential of MSEs to grow and to provide more and better jobs.

ILO/SEED RESEARCH PAPERS COMMISSIONED FOR THIS PROJECT

COUNTRY PAPERS

Chile

Espinosa, M. 2001. *Informe final encuesta a micro y pequeñas empresas (SEED): El caso de Chile*, unpublished SEED background paper, December (Santiago).

Flores, C. Forthcoming. *Creating a conducive policy environment for employment creation in MSEs in Chile*, SEED Working Paper (Geneva).

Roman, E. 2001. *Buenas políticas para la generación de buenos puestos de trabajo*, unpublished SEED background paper, July (Santiago).

Guinea

Kourouma, M. 2001. *Examen empirique des facteurs determinants du développement des micro et petites entreprises et de la stimulation des emplois en Guinée*, unpublished SEED background paper, December (Geneva).

——. 2003. *Promouvoir un environnement de développement des micro et petites entreprises guinéennes favorable à la création d'emplois décents*, SEED Working Paper No. 54 (Geneva).

Pakistan

Gallup/BRB Pakistan. 2003. *The influence of the policy and legal environment on micro and small enterprises in Pakistan. A survey of 333 micro and small enterprises*, SEED Working Paper (Geneva).

SMEDA. 2002. *Creating a conducive policy environment for micro, small and medium-sized enterprises in Pakistan*, SEED Working Paper No. 29 (Geneva).

Peru

Chacaltana, J. 2001. *Políticas públicas y empleo en las pequeñas y microempresas en el Perú* (Lima).

Ministerio de Trabajo y Promoción Social. 2001. *Encuesta de Micro y Pequeña Empresa (Informe de Avance)*, unpublished SEED background paper, October (Geneva).

South Africa

Mollentz, J. 2002. *Creating a conducive policy environment for employment creation in SMMEs in South Africa*, SEED Working Paper No. 35 (Geneva).

Pharoah, R.; Burton, P. 2001. *Evaluation of the International Labour Organisation's Start and Improve Your Business Programme in South Africa*, unpublished SEED background paper, November (Geneva/Johannesburg, ILO/DRA Development).

United Republic of Tanzania

Chijoriga, M.; Olomi, D.; Mwaipopo, L. 2002. *The influence of national policies, laws and regulations on employment in micro and small enterprises*, unpublished SEED background paper, November (Geneva/Dar es Salaam, ILO/University of Dar es Salaam).

Tibandebage, P. et al. 2003. *Creating a conducive policy environment for employment creation in micro and small enterprises in Tanzania*, SEED Working Paper No. 55 (Geneva).

Viet Nam

Pham, T.T.H; Nguyen, T.H.; Tran, C.D. 2002. *Survey on micro and small enterprises in Viet Nam. Survey report*, unpublished SEED background paper, May (Geneva/Hanoi, ILO/Viet Nam Chamber of Commerce and Industry).

——. 2002. *Creating a conducive environment for employment creation in small enterprises in Viet Nam*, SEED Working Paper No. 31 (Geneva).

THEMATIC PAPERS

Christensen, J.D.; Goedhuys, M. Forthcoming. *Impact of national policy and legal environments on employment growth and investment in micro and small enterprises*, SEED Working Paper (Geneva).

Goedhuys, M. 2002. *Employment creation and employment quality in African manufacturing firms*, SEED Working Paper No. 26 (Geneva).

Reinecke, G. 2002. *Small enterprises, big challenges. A literature review on the impact of the policy environment on the creation and improvement of jobs within small enterprises*, SEED Working Paper No. 23 (Geneva).

Xtenina, O. 2000. *Estimation of policy-induced factor price differences between small and large enterprises*, unpublished SEED background paper, May (Geneva).

For more details visit the ILO/SEED website: http://www.ilo.org/seed

ABBREVIATIONS

AGUIPE	Agence Guinéenne pour la Promotion de l'Emploi (Guinea)
BCRP	Banco Central de Reserva del Perú (Peru)
CASEN	Encuesta de Caracterización Socioeconómica Nacional (Chile)
DLW	Directorate of Labour Welfare
DNI	Direction Nationale des Impôts (Guinea)
ENAHO	Encuesta Nacional de Hogares (Peru)
EOBI	Employees Old Age Benefit Institution (Pakistan)
EPB	Export Promotion Bureau (Pakistan)
EPZ	Export processing zone
EsSalud	Entidad administradora del Seguro Social de Salud (Peru)
ESSI	Employment Social Security Institution (Pakistan)
GDP	Gross domestic product
GEAR	Growth Employment and Redistribution (South Africa)
GNP	Gross national product
ILO	International Labour Organization
ILO/SEED	InFocus Programme on boosting employment through Small EnterprisE Development
KILM	Key Indicators of the Labour Market
MSE	Micro- and small enterprise

MSME	Micro-, small and medium-sized enterprise
OECD	Organisation for Economic Co-operation and Development
OLS	Ordinary Least Squares
OPIP	Office de Promotion des Investissements Privés (Guinea)
PPF/NSSF	Employment Fund (United Republic of Tanzania)
RDP	Reconstruction and Development Programme (South Africa)
RER	Régimen Especial del Impuesto a la Renta (Chile)
RPED	Regional Program on Enterprise Development (World Bank)
RUR	Régimen Unico Simplificado (Chile)
RUT	Rol Unico Tributario (Chile)
SBP	Single Business Permit (Kenya)
SECP	Securities and Exchange Commission of Pakistan (Pakistan)
SME	Small and medium-sized enterprise
SMEDA	Small and medium-sized enterprise development authority (Pakistan)
SMME	Small, micro- and medium-sized enterprise
SUNAT	Superintendencia National de Administración Tributaria (Peru)
TRA	Tanzania Revenue Authority
VAT	Value added tax

INTRODUCTION

1

1.1 What is this book about?

The development of micro- and small enterprises (MSEs) can directly contribute to employment creation and poverty reduction.[1] Recognizing this, many governments in developing countries have made efforts to support such enterprises. Yet, millions of people around the world work in MSEs where they receive low incomes, lack social protection and work in dangerous conditions. At the root of this contradiction lies a policy and regulatory environment that should aid the development of MSEs and improve the quality of employment within them, but in practice often creates biases and stifles development.

The paradox of positive MSE promotion in the context of a biased and stifling environment

In this book, we take a critical look at the environments in which MSEs operate in a selection of developing countries, analysing their policies on MSE promotion, taxation, trade and finance, and their business and labour laws. By highlighting the strengths and weaknesses of specific policies and regulations and their interplay, we show how the MSE environment can be adapted and improved to make it more conducive to the growth of these enterprises and the quality and number of jobs they create. Aimed at policy-makers, development practitioners and researchers, this book will aid these and other stakeholders to enable MSEs to make an important contribution to reducing poverty.

---

[1] In this book, we refer to enterprises with between one and nine workers as micro-enterprises, and those between 10 and 49 workers as small enterprises (see box 1.1).

Background research was carried out in seven developing countries

The research which forms the backbone of our discussion was commissioned and supported by the ILO's InFocus Programme on boosting employment through Small EnterprisE Development (SEED), and carried out by national consultants or research institutions in seven developing countries: Chile, Guinea, Pakistan, Peru, South Africa, the United Republic of Tanzania and Viet Nam.[2] Each country study includes a mapping and analysis of policies and laws, an analysis of employment and establishment data, stakeholder interviews and workshops, and a survey of approximately 300 MSEs (see box 1.1 for the definition of MSEs used) to analyse their response to the policy and legal environment.[3] While the seven countries under study are very different in terms of their economic, political and social systems, this research identified a number of common issues within national policy and legal environments that influence – either directly or indirectly – the employment situation in MSEs. Thus, the findings presented here have a potential for application that goes well beyond our sample.

Putting employment creation and employment quality at the centre of analysis

A careful review of previous studies preceded the design of the research framework (see Reinecke, 2002). Several books have dealt with the policy environment for small enterprises and its impact on the dynamism of the small enterprise sector (see, for example, Stewart et al., 1990; Morrisson et al., 1994; English and Hénault, 1995; Snodgrass and Biggs, 1996). The influential study by de Soto (1989) sparked a whole series of studies that looked at the time and money required to register a small enterprise. However, these studies do not place employment creation and employment quality at the centre of analysis. The ILO, on the other hand, has published several studies that deal with small enterprise topics from the point of view of employment. These generally focus on micro-enterprises[4] and deal with one region or subregion only, but their main conceptual approaches and findings are important

---

[2] The selection of these seven countries, representing different regions and levels of socio-economic development, was based on several criteria, including the availability of statistical data and national researchers, as well as the current involvement of ILO/SEED in the country to ensure adequate follow-up. These criteria, while not applied rigidly, guided the selection of countries and enabled us to undertake a comparative analysis.

[3] A full list of the research papers prepared for this study is reproduced on pages xxi–xxii.

[4] This focus on micro-enterprises is suggested by the concept of the "informal sector", used in most of these studies. More recently, the debate has changed toward the broader concept of "informal economy" (ILO, 2002b), as we discuss further in box 3.1, Chapter 3.

Box 1.1   Defining micro- and small enterprises

While several international agencies have proposed their definitions of micro-, small and medium-sized enterprises, none of these definitions is universally accepted. The criteria used in defining enterprise size classes can include the number of workers and employees, as well as the size of turnover, value added or capital assets of enterprises. Some definitions are based on only one of these criteria, while others use several of them in combination.

The differences in definitions across countries are enormous. As a result, an enterprise that is considered a small enterprise in one country could be considered medium-sized or large in another country. For example, in Nicaragua, enterprises with more than 30 employees are considered "large", while in Mexico, manufacturing enterprises with 17 to 100 employees are considered "small".

In this book, the term "micro- and small enterprise (MSE)" shall refer to non-agricultural enterprises. For the purpose of data comparison or in the absence of a national definition, enterprises with one to nine workers are considered micro-enterprises, while those with ten to 49 workers are considered small enterprises. Self-employed workers are considered as micro-enterprises within this definition. When drawing from the policy assessments in the commissioned country reports, existing national definitions generally apply.

Sources: ILO/SEED and joint inquiry by KILM and SEED on available statistical data by enterprise size class.

ingredients for this book (for example, Klein and Tokman, 1996; Maldonado et al., 1999; Tokman et al., 2001).

The research findings presented here describe ways in which the role of government and other stakeholders in enterprise development and job creation can be made more effective and more sustainable. By improving the conditions in which enterprises of all sizes operate, national economies will benefit from a more diverse private sector, a more competitive and efficient economy, and a broader base of new employment opportunities.

1.2 The employment challenge: A reason for small enterprise promotion?

At the outset of the new millennium, there were 160 million unemployed people worldwide and 530 million working poor.[5] Nothing, in fact, is more fundamental to poverty reduction in

---

[5] This estimate is based on a one US$ per day poverty line. Although this indicator is limited by the fact that it only considers monetary income and neglects other dimensions of poverty, it is used internationally as a convenient indicator (ILO, 2002c).

the world than more and better employment (ILO, 2002c). Millions live in poverty because jobs of bad quality did not protect them against accidents and illnesses. Clearly, this is a challenge for employment promotion – but is it a reason to focus on small enterprises?

Shifting the focus from large to small enterprises

At first sight, large enterprises appear an attractive target for employment creation, precisely because they generate more employment by enterprise unit. For a time, public enterprises provided a significant source of employment in many countries. These enterprises were owned by the State to ensure their accountability and to enhance the social benefits they could create for the country. However, over the last decades the efficiency of state-owned enterprises has been called into question. Governments have faced greater demands from the population, and increasing competition in the world economy has meant that state ownership of enterprises has become less and less viable. The consequent privatization and downsizing of many state-owned enterprises have caused a rapid decline in employment in this type of enterprise.

Large private enterprises, whether domestically owned and operated or part of a multinational conglomerate, have also been affected by rapid market changes. These changes have required enterprises to operate more efficiently and competitively. The previous advantages of size, such as large stock inventories, hierarchical staff structures, and financial reserves, have been reassessed. Just-in-time stock management, flatter organizational structures, and diversified investments have become common. In order to remain competitive, many large enterprises have been fragmented into smaller units and subcontracting arrangements have become more common. As a result, employment within large enterprises has declined.

MSEs as important providers of employment

Over the last two decades, attention has turned to the capacity of MSEs to provide jobs. In numerical terms, the role of smaller enterprises as providers of employment is well documented. Our own research confirms this: in all seven countries studied, MSEs have been found to provide the majority of non-agricultural employment. There have also been indications that their relative significance could be growing. Between 1990 and 1998 in Latin America, for example, the employment share of self-employed and enterprises with up to 20 workers in total urban employment increased from

48 per cent to 51 per cent (ILO, 1999a). In our sample countries, increases in the MSE share of total employment have tended to be during recessions rather than economic upturns, suggesting that MSEs may have grown in response to the employment losses in larger enterprises and the public sector, or simply to a lack of employment alternatives.[6]

The share of female employment is much higher in MSEs than in larger enterprises in the countries under study. Many of these women will be working in MSEs in jobs of rather poor quality, but an increasing number are establishing their own dynamic, modern and successful MSEs. Improving the job quality for women in MSEs and realizing the potential of women-owned enterprises can make an important contribution to poverty eradication and socio-economic development.

The sheer size of the MSE sector demands attention from both policy-makers and development practitioners. Policies that are relevant only to large enterprises may fail to make a significant impact on the broader population. Just as the MSE sector contributes the majority of employment in all the countries studied, so improvements in the conditions in which MSEs operate can contribute to national economic and social development.

Poverty reduction and the promotion of employment is a central concern for governments around the world and often entails a combination of social and economic portfolios. While convention has often placed employment matters within labour portfolios, the promotion of employment is usually linked to the growth of the economy and broader economic arenas. As a result, governments often have a wide range of social and economic policy instruments with which to encourage the creation of new jobs. Despite this, the successful promotion of employment remains illusive. There appears to be no easy or replicable formula that can be universally applied. Governments have found that they cannot create jobs alone, but must work with other actors in the national economy. With the increasing speed of globalization, governments are also required to respond to the demands of the world economy and to work with new actors located

Combating poverty or making very poor people a little less poor?

---

[6] It should be noted, however, that most of the MSE owner-managers who took part in the surveys view launching an enterprise as a positive choice rather than a survival strategy.

beyond their national boundaries. Governments have to balance a broad array of influences on their economy so that national policy-making occurs with an eye on what the rest of the world is doing.

Many organizations working in the field of small enterprise development have based their work, implicitly or explicitly, on two key assumptions. First, that a thriving MSE sector contributes to the overall growth of employment, and second, that the design and implementation of a conducive policy environment for MSEs promotes the growth of jobs in these enterprises and improvements in the quality of those jobs. However, as we have suggested, employment within MSEs may sometimes simply replace those jobs that were lost from large enterprises. Furthermore, a growing share of employment within MSEs is not an end in itself and cannot be the main criterion for assessing the success of MSE policies. Job quality in the MSE sector is generally low. In many countries, huge numbers of new MSEs are being established in times of economic crisis by persons who do not have any alternative, which is obviously not in itself an indicator of successful socio-economic development. In other words, these enterprises can be very important in "helping a large number of very poor people become a little less poor" (Mead and Liedholm, 1998, p. 70), but they often do not provide employment of sufficient quality to be a path out of poverty.

Enabling MSEs to create jobs of better quality

The biggest challenge facing policy-makers is to enable MSEs to create jobs of better quality. Improving the quality of employment in MSEs requires policy initiatives that are responsive to the needs and capabilities of workers and employers, while also setting goals and standards that are acceptable both domestically and internationally. Since its inception, the ILO has endeavoured to work with member States to assist them in the design, implementation and management of such policies. While the promotion of job quality has often involved the regulation of labour standards through collaboration between governments, large employer associations and mass labour movements in large industrial and public sector settings, the emergence of the MSE sector requires a new understanding of job quality within a more diverse and fragmented range of employers and workers. Government policy, therefore, needs to respond to these changes – keeping track of the reality of the workforce and the marketplace, while promoting better standards and conditions for all.

In sum, no employment strategy can be successful if it does not take small enterprises into account. However, small enterprise development is not a goal in itself. Nor is an increasing share of small enterprise employment in total employment an indicator of success. Rather, we see small enterprise development as a strategy contributing to poverty eradication and better employment opportunities for women and men, both as individuals and groups or cooperatives. The success of this strategy could be measured by increasing job quality in MSEs and a high rate of graduation of MSEs to medium-sized and large enterprises.

1.3 From enterprise promotion to an enabling environment

Enterprises of all size classes, from micro to large, are the main creators of employment. These economic units provide products or services while generating jobs and wealth. Enabling MSEs to thrive and create more employment is an attractive policy avenue, therefore, but one which need not be restricted to policies of direct promotion. Only a small minority of MSEs benefit from targeted promotion, while all enterprises are affected by a wide range of economic policies, the intended and unintended consequences of which can have a big impact on MSEs. It is thus important to have a broad and integrated perspective as we look at the impact of policies on MSEs and consider how to reform this environment (Meier and Pilgrim, 1994; Snodgrass and Biggs, 1996).

The importance of an integrated perspective

The key role of private enterprise as a vehicle for job creation often leads governments and development institutions into the business development arena. Development services and support programmes are provided to help enterprises improve their competitiveness and enhance their potential to retain or expand their employment base. Governments have introduced programmes that use enterprise development as a means to reduce poverty and have specifically designed programmes to help unemployed people establish their own businesses.

Development programmes have limited impact

Over time, the validity, effectiveness and sustainability of these development programmes have been questioned. Very few enterprises benefited from these schemes. Moreover, many programmes did not match the real needs and demands of enterprises and, through subsidies, contributed to the distortion of markets and the marginalization of the small enterprise sector. Some governments allocate considerable funding to support small enterprise development by targeted groups, such as women entrepreneurs, but this assistance is delivered via a welfare approach, rather than through support for the enterprise. Previous investigations into these programmes have fuelled a debate concerning the role of government in business development, which has also drawn attention to the broader environment in which MSEs operate (Committee of Donor Agencies for Small Enterprise Development, 1997 and 2001).

Policy biases against MSEs

Despite the importance of small enterprises in employment, most policy and legal environments favour larger enterprises over smaller ones. Large enterprises, including foreign-owned and multinational corporations, tend to benefit from government-provided incentives or exemptions, while their smaller siblings are either not eligible for these opportunities or unable to make use of them because of procedural barriers.

Moreover, small enterprises suffer more than larger ones from a lack of transparency in the implementation of laws and regulations. They are more likely than larger enterprises to find it necessary to make irregular payments to government officials, and these payments represent a larger proportion of their revenues than is the case for larger enterprises (World Bank, 2001). Thus, the policy and legal environment is often more conducive to the establishment and operation of larger enterprises than of smaller ones.

ILO recognition of the need for an enabling environment

The ILO has recognized the need for an enabling policy environment for small enterprises. In 1998, the International Labour Conference adopted the Job Creation in Small and Medium-Sized Enterprises Recommendation (No. 189). This Recommendation recognizes the importance of setting a conducive policy and legal environment for small enterprise development and encourages governments to ensure that enterprises of all size classes enjoy equal opportunities as regards the access to such elements as credit and foreign

Box 1.2   Job Creation in Small and Medium-sized Enterprises Recommendation, 1998 (No. 189)

By adopting Recommendation No. 189, entitled General conditions to stimulate job creation in small and medium enterprises, the Members of the ILO – governments, employers' organizations and workers' organizations – have recognized the fundamental role that small enterprises can play in promoting full, productive and freely chosen employment. Although not legally binding, the Recommendation reflects the commitment of ILO Members to small enterprise development.

The Recommendation provides guidance for the development of an enterprise culture and an effective service infrastructure, as well as for a conducive policy environment. It encourages member States to "adopt and pursue appropriate fiscal, monetary and employment policies to promote an optimal economic environment" and to design policies promoting efficient and competitive small enterprises that provide productive and sustainable employment under adequate social conditions. To achieve this, it is necessary to create conditions that provide access to credit, foreign exchange and imported inputs and fair taxation. It is also necessary to provide effective labour laws and regulations to raise the quality of employment in small enterprises and compliance to international labour standards.

The text of the Recommendation also deals with the process of policy reform by encouraging Members to review the impact of existing policies and regulations on small and medium-sized enterprises, and to review labour and social legislation. This review, which should be carried out in consultation with organizations of employers and workers, will help to determine whether such legislation meets the needs of small and medium-sized enterprises, while ensuring adequate protection and working conditions for their workers.

exchange, as described in box 1.2. This book can be used as a tool to facilitate the review and reform of the policy environment in view of creating more and better employment, as the Recommendation advises.

In terms of policy choices, the predominant opinion found within the literature reviewed is that there are no generally valid reasons for economic policies to favour any specific size class of enterprises. In order to provide a "level playing field" for enterprises of all size classes, policies can foster the development of well-functioning markets that are not biased against MSEs. This may require state interventions of various types, for example in the area of credit for small enterprises (Berry, 1995; Snodgrass and Biggs, 1996). Although some general recommendations on which policies should not be chosen may be derived from the literature, there is no uniform best practice for all policy areas.

In sum, the analysis of the impact of policies on employment creation by MSEs requires a comprehensive approach. Rather than focusing on MSE promotion policies, we consider various economic policies, laws and regulations and their impact on MSEs.

1.4 The comparative research project

1.4.1 Research questions and framework

In order to gain a better understanding of how policy environments within nations influence the generation and quality of employment within MSEs, three key research questions were formulated at the outset of the study:

1. **To what extent can the identified pattern of MSE employment be considered desirable in terms of socio-economic development?**
   This question was formulated to focus on the contribution MSEs make to employment within the national context, in terms of both the quantity and quality of employment. We wanted to specify those instances where MSEs were established merely as a by-product of a poor economy and a last resort – an initiative taken by individuals to prevent them from falling further into poverty – and those where MSE development may be a vehicle through which desirable forms of employment are pursued.

2. **What are the main elements of a well-designed policy and legal environment for MSE employment creation?**
   Here, the research focused on the policy and legal environment in which MSEs operate. Our concern centred on the nature of the connection between the policy and legal environment and the quantity and quality of employment to be found in MSEs. We wanted to identify key elements, traits or features of the policy and legal environment that can be considered conducive to "decent jobs" in the sector.[7]

---

[7] The concept of "decent work" is at the core of the ILO's Decent Work Agenda (ILO, 1999b), which aims to promote opportunities for women and men to obtain decent and productive work, in conditions of freedom, equity, security and human dignity. This overarching goal embraces four strategic objectives, namely promoting rights at work; the generation of employment and incomes; extending social protection and social security; and strengthening social dialogue.

3. What are the main elements required for effective implementation of policies and laws for MSEs?

Experience has taught us that passing policies and laws is only a part of the equation. Difficulties in enacting and implementing these instruments can often create outcomes that are quite different from the original intentions. This is why we have sought to identify those implementation strategies found to contribute to success.

While our research was primarily concerned with the policy and legal environment, it was recognized that this is not the only factor that matters. Rather, the policy and legal environment is one important part of the broader business environment for MSEs. The business environment in which MSEs operate is also shaped by many other elements, including market opportunities, the availability of resources and the cultural and social context, as well as the existence of institutions providing advice and information, such as associations, non-governmental organizations (NGOs) and trade unions.

The policy and legal environment is part of the broader business environment

The degree to which the business environment enables or constrains MSE activity is dependent on the combined impact of these functions. Moreover, the impact of the policy environment is not restricted to its direct impact on enterprise strategies, but also includes its indirect impact via other elements of the business environment. Finally, it is the cumulative impact of decisions made by individual MSE owner-managers[8] that leads to changes in the aggregate employment in the MSE sector.

Figure 1.1 illustrates the conceptual framework described. It shows a series of causal relationships that need to be better understood in order to assess the impact of the policy environment on the volume and quality of employment in MSEs. Unfortunately, there is no comprehensive research method that would allow us to assess all the relevant causal links identified. We have therefore used a range of comparative research methods to obtain relevant information in the seven countries under study.[9] A structured case study approach was adopted to generate findings that could be compared with one

---

[8] We use the term "owner-manager", as MSEs rarely exhibit a separation between ownership and management.

[9] For a discussion on the potential and limitations of international comparative research, see Verba (1967) and Sartori (1994).

Figure 1.1 Conceptual framework

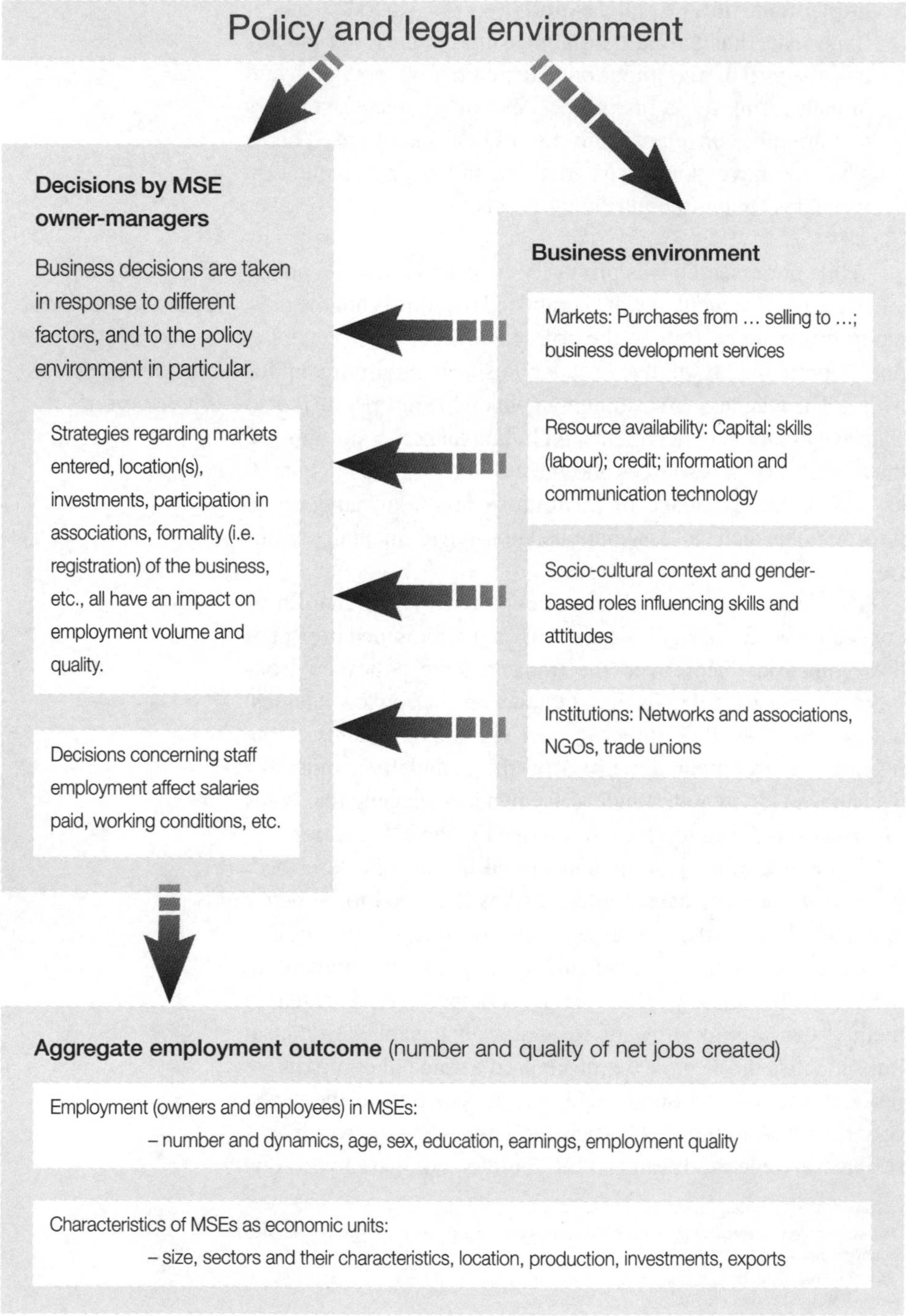

Policy and legal environment

Decisions by MSE owner-managers

Business decisions are taken in response to different factors, and to the policy environment in particular.

Strategies regarding markets entered, location(s), investments, participation in associations, formality (i.e. registration) of the business, etc., all have an impact on employment volume and quality.

Decisions concerning staff employment affect salaries paid, working conditions, etc.

Business environment

Markets: Purchases from ... selling to ...; business development services

Resource availability: Capital; skills (labour); credit; information and communication technology

Socio-cultural context and gender-based roles influencing skills and attitudes

Institutions: Networks and associations, NGOs, trade unions

Aggregate employment outcome (number and quality of net jobs created)

Employment (owners and employees) in MSEs:
– number and dynamics, age, sex, education, earnings, employment quality

Characteristics of MSEs as economic units:
– size, sectors and their characteristics, location, production, investments, exports

another wherever this was possible, while also capturing essential information particular to each country.

Data collection and analysis were carried out in steps. First, the aggregate employment outcome was analysed – that is, the number and quality of existing and new jobs in MSEs. Then, the policy environment was mapped and assessed to identify the characteristics that shape the decisions of business owner-managers. This included the assessment of the broader business environment in which MSEs operate. Finally, the link between the policy environment and the MSE employment outcome was assessed. Each of these steps is described in more detail below.

1.4.2 Analysis of the aggregate employment outcomes

Assessing the national aggregate employment changes involved three factors. The first was the volume of employment in MSEs. An overall picture of employment by enterprise size classes and its characteristics was sought to provide an initial insight into the role of MSEs in the economy and, in particular, as employers. Moreover, MSE employment was compared to employment in other enterprise size classes by characteristics such as age, gender, education, and, when appropriate, race or ethnicity.

Assessing the volume, flow and quality of MSE employment

The second factor was employment flows. National researchers were requested to assess wherever possible the amount of employment that was created by MSEs, by measuring employment over time in the MSE sector and according to enterprise size classes. Researchers focused on employment flows into and out of MSEs – assessing start-up rates and death rates, as well as the graduation and downsizing of enterprises.

The third factor investigated addressed the quality of employment in MSEs. This area of investigation examined the earnings of MSE owners and their employees and compared these to earnings in larger enterprises. Other aspects of employment quality were also investigated wherever data could be found. This included working conditions, employment status, the prevalence of written work contracts, and the participation of employees in social protection schemes, MSE associations and trade unions. For each of these job quality aspects, a comparison with the situation in large enterprises was undertaken.

1.4.3 Mapping and assessing the policy environment

Six policy fields
for analysis

For the analysis of the policy and legal environment, we selected six policy fields: specific small enterprise policies, business laws and regulations, taxation, labour policy, trade, and finance. Each of these policy fields has some impact on the employment situation for MSEs because they influence the decisions that entrepreneurs make, including decisions regarding employment. The aggregate employment outcome in terms of the volume and quality of employment created by MSEs depends on entrepreneurs' strategies in response to the environment they face: it is individual entrepreneurs who make decisions in terms of starting up the business, hiring workers, setting wages and determining other working conditions.

The assessment of the broader business environment covered other factors that directly affect the decisions of the owner-manager. The most prominent factor is market opportunities. Overall market fluctuations, changes in prices and quality, and "niche markets" identified obviously have a strong impact on MSEs. The availability of resources also plays an important role: the access to credit, skills and information can influence the decisions that an entrepreneur takes. Another factor is the cultural and social context in which business owner-managers are located, as well as gender-based roles and relations, which can have a significant impact upon their decisions. In some cases, "traditional" cultures may constrain enterprises where, for example, women are disadvantaged or discouraged from starting a business. Alternatively, there may exist an entrepreneurial culture which rewards and encourages entrepreneurship. Finally, the degree of access that business owner-managers have to advice and business training and their participation in chambers of commerce or business associations represent external factors that can influence their decisions. The presence of networks, NGOs and business associations is thus an important element of MSEs' business environment.

The national consultants commissioned for this research were required to comprehensively map the policies and laws that could be found in the six policy areas. Such a mapping is crucial, because in many countries not even governments are aware of all the regulations an enterprise has to face (Jansson,

Box 1.3   The MSE surveys

In each of the seven countries under study, ILO/SEED commissioned a survey of approximately 300 micro- and small enterprises. The survey was designed to analyse the response of MSE owners and managers to the policy and legal environment. The samples for the surveys included MSEs with two to 49 workers and were stratified by size (micro/small), location (rural/urban), economic sector (manufacturing/commerce/services) and gender. Self-employed workers, while included in the analysis of employment data and policy assessment, were excluded from the samples (see the Annex for further details on the samples and reasons for the sampling strategy used).

2000). Each of these policies and laws was evaluated using an assessment matrix provided by ILO/SEED. Expert assessments by the national consultants or key informants and focus group discussions were used to assess the broader business environment. Finally, a survey of approximately 300 MSE owner-managers was used in each of the seven countries to assess the relative importance of the policy areas and the broader business environment in their employment decisions (box 1.3).

1.4.4 Assessing the impact of the policy and legal environment

The assessment of the impact of the policy and legal environment on employment in the MSE sector was undertaken at various levels. At the national level, the assessment sought to determine the impact of each policy field on MSE employment, as well as the overall impact the combination of these policies had on employment. Unfortunately, research on the causal relationship between policy environments and employment outcomes is inherently difficult because of the multitude of factors involved and the methodological problems in measuring them.

In order to determine the impact of laws and regulations under these circumstances, we used a range of comparisons: *Comparisons used*

*   Careful cross-country comparison of the policy environment and the employment situation in the seven countries. The mapping and assessing enabled us to carry out systematic (rather than anecdotal) comparison.

- Comparisons over time within one country, especially in those cases where policies and laws had experienced drastic changes over the 1990s.

- Comparisons between the employment performance of enterprises with different degrees of compliance with legal and regulatory requirements.

- Comparison between different regions within one country, especially in the case of substantial local or regional variations in the policy and legal environment.

At the micro-level, the MSE surveys were used to gain an insight into entrepreneurial perceptions of the policy and legal environment, as well as the impact this factor had on their decisions regarding employment (volume and quality) in their enterprise. Although necessarily based on owners' and managers' subjective assessment, these surveys were designed to identify factors in the policy and legal environment that directly influenced decisions.

1.5 The structure of this book

Chapter 2 deals with the role of policy in small enterprise employment. This includes research findings on how changes in the policy environment were found to influence employment in the MSE sector. The two elements of quantity and quality of employment in MSEs are addressed. Chapter 3 presents ways in which compliance with regulations can be used as a means of developing the MSE sector. We examine the issue of informality and present the continuum of compliance and formality. Chapter 4 reviews the six selected policy fields that make up the policy and legal environment in the countries under study. Based on these findings, Chapter 5 discusses concrete steps for stakeholders to take to reform the policy environment. It also discusses the role of technical assistance in this field. Finally, the Annex provides additional statistical data and technical information on the methodological approaches employed in this research.

THE ROLE OF POLICY IN SMALL ENTERPRISE EMPLOYMENT

2

Employment in the MSE sector is closely connected to macro-level policy. We have found that changes in the policy environment – especially in the macroeconomic development strategies employed – have affected MSEs directly and indirectly in all the countries investigated. In some cases, these changes have been intentional and beneficial. Unfortunately, in the majority of cases, these changes have been unintentional and have resulted in employment in MSEs that is of inferior quality compared to other enterprises.

The policy environment affects MSEs directly and indirectly
The paradox of positive MSE promotion in the context of a biased and stifling environment

Unlike in medium-sized and large enterprises, the decision-making processes within MSEs usually rest with one person: the owner-manager. The policy and legal framework can directly affect the decisions of this woman or man through rules and incentives that prescribe or encourage certain kinds of behaviours. Business licences – such as licences for the production of food, for example – set rules that require owner-managers to achieve a certain standard in their production processes. Export rebates, on the other hand, provide financial incentives to owner-managers to sell their products in foreign markets. While larger enterprises also respond to the policy environment, their decision process is different because administrative and technical staff are available to study regulations and take appropriate action. For MSEs, the availability of information to individual owner-managers is thus a crucial determinant of the direct impact of laws and regulations.

Owner-managers can also be affected by indirect relationships with national policies and laws. Although sometimes harder to identify, these relationships are no less significant than those that are direct. National policies and laws can influence the decisions of various actors in the market, which can in turn affect the decisions of other actors. A national policy that reduces public sector enterprises and retrenches many workers, for example, obliges these workers to find employment elsewhere. This policy change can force many unemployed women and men to consider self-employment or micro-enterprise as a survival strategy, which in turn may increase competition and affect the profitability in sectors where many MSEs operate. Thus, policy change in one field has created change in another.

Another source of indirect policy influences can be found in policies that affect product and input markets. It is this field of policy that we have found to be one of the most potent. When surveying around 300 MSEs in each of the seven countries studied, our researchers found that MSE owner-managers perceive market forces as the most significant source of influence over their employment decisions. Based on their understanding of input and product markets, MSE owner-managers take decisions to expand or reduce their workforce. They also decide to improve the conditions, remuneration or skills of their work-force according to perceived market factors. As we will show in this chapter, well-functioning markets do not come about spontaneously but rather depend on various institutional arrangements and policy interventions. This is all the more so for MSEs, which often suffer from restricted access to product and input markets. Thus, there is a critical connection between national policies and laws and the markets in which MSEs operate.

We examine the relationship between the national policy framework and MSE employment in three steps. First, we examine the contribution MSEs make to employment in the seven countries studied, and identify the influence the national policy framework has had on these employment patterns. Second, we go beyond the issue of employment volumes and assess the quality of employment found in MSEs. While employment quality can be difficult to measure, it is essential that the promotion of new employment opportunities incorporate a consideration of the quality of these jobs. Here again, the relationship between job quality in the MSE sector and the national policy framework will be discussed. We conclude by examining the twin impact of policies and markets on MSEs in order to clarify the various relationships found between policies, laws and regulations and the decisions of enterprise owner-managers.

2.1 The policy environment and employment in MSEs

2.1.1 The contribution of MSEs to employment and GDP

Micro- and small enterprises account for 97.5 to 99.7 per cent of all enterprises in the countries under study.[1] Figure 2.1 shows the employment share of MSEs in non-agricultural employment for the seven countries under study and for the European Union, which can be used as a benchmark for developed countries. Unfortunately, these data are not directly comparable across countries; in some cases, they refer to the informal economy, and, by excluding the upper segment of small enterprises, they underestimate the true participation of MSEs in the labour market. However, they illustrate the high proportion of employment that is found in MSEs in these countries. MSEs also make a substantial contribution to the gross domestic product (GDP) in most countries, although their share in GDP is lower than their share in employment, reflecting a lower productivity of MSEs compared to larger enterprises.[2]

The majority of non-agricultural employment is in MSEs

In all seven countries under study, the MSE survey results show that micro-enterprises often grow and that their employment growth rates are fairly high. Although micro-enterprises grow fast, their growth path is short. The growth rates drop quickly as enterprises move to a slightly larger size, turning negative as enterprises reach the size of about ten workers. Relatively few enterprises attain a size of ten or more paid workers. For example, between 2 per cent (South Africa) and 5 per cent (Chile) of the sample enterprises with three to four paid employees in 1999 had increased their employment level to ten or more paid workers by 2001. The proportion of expanding MSEs was fairly similar between enterprises owned

---

[1] See the Annex for more detailed data and technical notes.
[2] See figure A.1 in the Annex for more detail.

Figure 2.1 Share of micro- and small enterprises in non-agricultural employment, most recent data

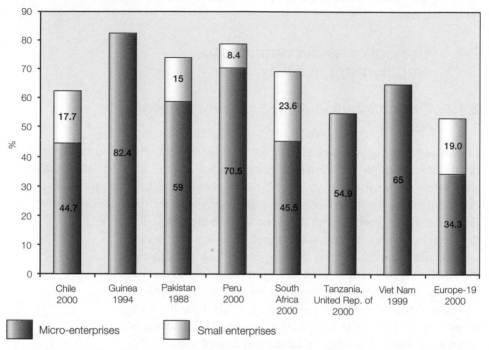

Notes: MSEs include self-employed persons. For a definition of MSEs in the different countries, see the Annex. Guinea and the United Republic of Tanzania: due to lack of data availability, informal sector employment has been used as a proxy for MSE employment. Guinea: urban informal sector employment as a share of non-agricultural employment. The United Republic of Tanzania: informal sector employment as a share of non-agricultural employment. Peru: share of MSEs in urban employment. Viet Nam: share of private sector, which includes formal private enterprises and semi-informal household enterprises, in total employment. Europe-19 includes the EU-countries, Iceland, Liechtenstein, Norway and Switzerland and refers to non-primary private employment.

Sources: Country papers and European Commission (2002).

Women tend to be concentrated in micro-enterprises

by women and those owned by men (Christensen and Goedhuys, forthcoming).

In most of the countries studied, it has been difficult to obtain data on MSE employment shares that distinguish between men and women. In several countries, such data are simply not collected on a regular basis. However, from the data available it is obvious that MSEs are especially important as employment providers for women. In most countries, the share of women in MSE employment is much higher than their share among medium-sized and large enterprises. Unfortunately, these employment opportunities are often concentrated in the most fragile segment of survivalist micro-enterprises, where incomes tend to be very low. For example, while women account for

47 per cent of own-account workers and micro-enterprise employment in Peru, their share is 38 per cent in small enterprises and only 30 per cent in medium-sized and large enterprises.[3] A similar pattern is found for Chile. Although available statistical data are not always comparable across countries, they confirm the importance of MSEs as employment providers for women in the African countries under study and in Viet Nam as well.[4]

Women-owned enterprises within the MSE sector are represented most highly among micro-enterprises, and, as the size of enterprises grows, the proportion of women-owned enterprises declines. For example, in the Tanzanian informal sector, 38 per cent of the enterprises without employees are run by women, while this share is only 19 per cent for enterprises with five to nine employees.[5] This is partly the result of discriminatory policies in the fields of education and training, which have limited women's access to further education and vocational skills training, as well as a reflection of women's restricted access to the levels of finance required for business expansion rather than microfinance. This is another illustration of how policies in apparently unrelated areas can have distorting effects on enterprise policies.

Obtaining employment and establishment data for the seven countries that can be compared across different time periods has also proven difficult. However, the available evidence suggests that, with the exception of Chile, the employment share in MSEs is increasing over time.[6] In itself, this is neither good nor bad news, but it does justify the focus on the environment in which these enterprises operate, as well as on the quality of these jobs. The significant and increasing contribution of MSEs can be explained as a result of the impact of the national policy framework. In some cases, national policies have targeted MSEs and sought to develop them further. However, in most cases, employment in MSEs is a result of broader macroeconomic policies that affect the operation of the whole economy and subsequently have influenced the MSE sector.

---

[3] Data refer to the year 2000 and cover private employment in Lima.

[4] See Pham (2002, p. 27) for Viet Nam, and Charmes (1999) and ILO (2002e) for the African countries and an international overview. In Pakistan, female participation in MSEs was much lower (SMEDA, 2002, p. 17).

[5] Authors' calculations based on data from the 1991 Informal Sector Survey. Evidence from Latin America also suggests that on average, women-owned firms are smaller and younger than their male-owned counterparts (Inter-American Development Bank, 2001).

[6] See table A.3 in the Annex.

2.1.2 The link between MSE employment and the policy environment

Economic liberalization increases the role and employment share of MSEs

In many of the countries studied, evidence was found to link public policies with changes in national employment patterns. Changes in a country's development strategy and macro-economic policies have a clear impact on the volume of employment in MSE. In particular, policies of economic liberalization caused an increase of the MSE share in non-agricultural employment. This was found in the context of transitional economies such as the United Republic of Tanzania and Viet Nam, as well as within established market economies such as Peru and South Africa.

The seven countries under study differ in terms of their political systems, socio-economic development and labour market situation. Table 2.1 and table 2.2 give a quick overview of some key economic and social indicators.

In terms of the broad economic strategies that were predominant in the seven countries over the 1990s, three groups of countries can be distinguished. The first group consists of countries that have been in transition from a socialist economy

Table 2.1   Overview of basic economic and social indicators in all seven countries, 2000

	GDP per capita (PPP$) 2000	GDP per capita annual growth rate (percentages) 1990–2000	Human Development Index 2000 (rank in brackets)
Chile	9 417	5.2	0.831 (38)
Guinea	1 982	1.7	0.414 (159)
Pakistan	1 928	1.2	0.499 (138)
Peru	4 799	2.9	0.747 (82)
South Africa	9 401	−0.6	0.695 (107)
Tanzania, United Rep. of	523	0.1	0.440 (151)
Viet Nam	1 996	6.0	0.688 (109)
High-income countries	27 639	1.7	0.93
Middle-income countries	5 734	2.4	0.747
Low-income countries	2 002	1.2	0.554
World	7 446	1.2	0.722

Notes: PPP$ = purchasing-power parity dollars. Human Development Index 2000 ranks countries out of 173.

Sources: UNDP (2002), Mollentz (2002), and Stats SA.

Table 2.2   Employment share by sector in all seven countries, most recent year
(percentages)

	Agriculture	Industry	Trade and services
Chile (2002)	13.1	24.1	62.8
Guinea (1987)	84.8	..	n.a.
Pakistan (1999/2000)	48.5	18.0	33.5
Peru (2000)	32.4	14.4	53.2
South Africa (2000)	26.5	22.4	51.1
Tanzania, United Rep. of (2000/01)	82.1	2.6	15.3
Viet Nam (1998)	67.1	12.8	20.2

Note: .. = not available.

Sources: Chile: Encuesta Nacional de Empleo; Guinea: Kourouma (2003); Pakistan: ILO Laborstat based on Labour Force Survey; Peru: Encuesta Nacional de Hogares (ENAHO); South Africa: Mollentz (2002); the United Republic of Tanzania: Labour Force Survey 2000/2001; Viet Nam: General Statistical Office, Viet Nam Living Standards Survey, 1997–1998 (Hanoi, 2000).

toward a market economy. This is the case in Guinea, the United Republic of Tanzania and Viet Nam. The second group consists of market economies that have carried out liberalization strategies to reduce the role of government in the production of goods and to strengthen private enterprises. Pakistan, Peru and South Africa were found to fall within this group of countries. Finally, Chile is the only country that had already undergone most market reforms at the outset of the 1990s. These three categories of economic change will be briefly described to highlight the connections that were found between national policy frameworks and the state of the MSE sector.

The experience of Guinea, the United Republic of Tanzania and Viet Nam illustrate to differing degrees how MSEs have become a part of the process of economic transition. Guinea is a West African country with abundant natural resources. As we can see from table 2.1, the level of human development is low, ranking 159th of 173 countries, according to the Human Development Index (UNDP, 2002). During the first decades after its independence in 1958, the country followed a socialist development strategy. In the mid-1970s, private enterprises of any size were prohibited. Starting in 1985, policies were introduced to move away from a socialist development strategy toward a more market-oriented approach. Private enterprise was permitted and a policy and legal framework for private commercial activity was established. Between 1990 and 2000, per capita GDP has grown

Transition from socialism and MSEs

by an annual average of 1.7 per cent, despite continued political instability. The inflation rate, which was as high as 72 per cent in 1986, was down to only 2 per cent in 1997.

The broader environment for private enterprises was also liberalized in Guinea over the last decade, reforming, for example, the tariff systems. However, in an effort to maintain sufficient levels of government revenues, there has been a recent increase in state charges, which may have contributed to the decision by many MSE owner-managers to remain hidden from the formal economy. There has been a strong increase in urban informal employment in Guinea, both in absolute terms and as a share of total non-agricultural employment (from 75 per cent in 1987 to 82 per cent in 1994).

In the United Republic of Tanzania, the Arusha Declaration of 1967 established a direction for socialist development in which private enterprise was severely restricted. However, the Economic Survival Programme of 1981/82 reversed this course and set in motion a process of liberalization of the national economy, which was reinforced by the Economic Recovery Programmes of 1986/89 and 1989/92. Since 1992, the Government has undertaken a rigorous public sector reform process that has reduced public sector employment from 355,000 in 1992 to 270,000 in 1998. In addition, more than half of the 400 state-owned enterprises have been privatized. Similarly to Guinea, the labour market is strongly dominated by agricultural employment.

Economic liberalization has resulted in an increased number of MSEs across the United Republic of Tanzania, and in micro-enterprises in particular. It is estimated that the number of micro-enterprises has increased at least threefold compared to the period prior to economic adjustment. According to the 2000/01 Household Budget Survey, some 42 per cent of households reported having a business (National Bureau of Statistics Tanzania, 2002, p. 60). As in Guinea, the majority of MSEs in the United Republic of Tanzania are found in the informal economy. There are no precise data on the evolution of employment by enterprise size, but data from the country's labour force surveys show that 61 per cent of households in urban areas had informal economy activities in 2000/01, as compared to 42 per cent in 1990/91 (National Bureau of Statistics Tanzania, 2003).

Economic reform policies in Viet Nam, which are called Doi Moi ("Renovation Policies") in Vietnamese, were introduced in 1986. This package of policy reforms has led Viet Nam toward a multi-sector economy in which private enterprises are able to operate alongside state-owned enterprises within a market-oriented environment. Since this time, significant growth in the private sector has been witnessed, including small and individually run businesses and household enterprises. Per capita GDP grew at an average of 6 per cent per year between 1990 and 2000, and the number of household enterprises expanded from 1 million in 1992 to 1.7 million in 1999.

Unlike many other countries, where the transition to a market economy has been accompanied by economic recessions and increasing rates of poverty, Viet Nam has achieved relatively strong growth and macroeconomic stability for most of the 1990s. The incidence of poverty has fallen from more than 70 per cent in the mid-1980s to about 37 per cent in 1998. Most employment growth has been generated in the informal and private sectors. The introduction of the Enterprise Law in 2000 contributed to a rapid acceleration in the registration of new businesses by lowering the time and money required to register. During the first year of enactment, 14,444 enterprises were newly registered under the Enterprise Law, more than twice as many as in 1999 under earlier legislation. By the end of 2001, some 35,000 enterprises had been newly registered under the Enterprise Law. Seventy per cent of these enterprises were found to be newly established.

MSEs in liberalizing market

We now turn to those countries that have been operating in a capitalist mode for some time, but have been engaged in processes that further liberalize their markets. Pakistan, Peru and South Africa are examples of countries where MSEs have been affected by liberalization of their market-oriented economies.

The removal of apartheid policies in 1994 and the liberalization of the economy in South Africa have contributed to the growth of small, micro- and medium-sized enterprises (SMMEs), with a high number of "survivalist" enterprises emerging.[7] The Reconstruction and Development Programme

---

[7] Survivalist enterprises are defined by the South African Enterprise Promotion Agency Ntsika as enterprises without paid employees and with negligible asset value, generating incomes below the minimum income standard or poverty line.

(RDP) was the first response of the new democratic Government to demands for socio-economic reform. It set new priorities for development that could be measured in terms of improvements to the quality of human life. The RDP recognized the role of small business in providing a direct and substantial contribution to a better quality of life. In 1996, the Government approved the Growth Employment and Redistribution (GEAR) policy as a macroeconomic framework for development, committing it to job creation through a more competitive and faster growing economy, the transition to greater flexibility and productivity in the labour market, and the investment by business in training and development initiatives.

These macroeconomic initiatives resulted in a growth of the private sector, particularly among MSEs. Small enterprises, for example, were found by Gumede (2000) to have strongly increased their share in manufacturing employment between 1988 and 1997. At the same time, however, unemployment rates are extremely high, forcing many unemployed people into entrepreneurial activities with low economic returns and weak perspectives of development. The strong increase in the employment share of unregistered economic activities in total employment, from 26 per cent in 1999 to 31 per cent in 2001 (Hussmanns and du Jeu, 2002), is one indicator of the importance of survivalist enterprises.

In Pakistan, the structure of the national economy has shifted over the last 50 years from agriculture to manufacturing, trade and services. In order to keep pace with the growing labour force, the Government has followed a plan of rapid industrialization. Most significant in this process has been the privatization of state-owned enterprises and other liberalization policies, which have strongly affected MSEs. Pakistan has also introduced stabilization and structural adjustment programmes that have led to reductions in public expenditure. Private sector development became recognized as the main engine of economic growth in the 1980s, as the Government sought to open its foreign exchange and promote exports, particularly in the manufacturing sector. These policy shifts contributed to an overall increase in GDP, which grew at an annual rate of 6.6 per cent during this decade, and in large-scale manufacturing, which expanded by 16.6 per cent a year from 1982 to 1988. The liberalization of the financial sector has resulted in the growth of commercial banks and leasing companies.

Consistent with the Government's focus on manufacturing enterprises in this period of macroeconomic reform in Pakistan, employment in manufacturing micro-enterprises has been found to increase at an average annual rate of more than 6 per cent from 1988 to 1997.[8] Furthermore, the Census of Establishments conducted in 1988 shows that almost 80 per cent of non-agricultural employment in Pakistan is generated by micro-, small and medium-sized enterprises.[9]

In Peru, the MSE sector has been affected by liberalization of the market-oriented economy in a more negative manner. Before 1990, the Peruvian economy was characterized by heavy state intervention in the form of price controls, import barriers, subsidies and tax exemptions. Labour laws were protective for workers, but only applied to a limited number of workers in the formal economy. These policies ran into a serious crisis in the late 1980s as the inflation rate reached 2,775 per cent in 1989 and the economy shrank by 12 per cent. This forced the Government to introduce a series of measures to stabilize the economy in 1990. Most price controls were abolished and the maximum rate of import tariffs was reduced from 84 per cent to 25 per cent between 1990 and 1991. These reforms resulted in a short period of strong economic growth from 1993 to 1995, but the rest of the 1990s was characterized again by strong economic and political turbulence.

This process of economic liberalization led to a sharp increase in the share of micro-enterprises in urban employment, rising from 71 per cent in 1990 to 78 per cent in Metropolitan Lima in 2000, while during the same period the share of large enterprises decreased from 22 per cent to 17 per cent. However, this increase in MSE employment was not an indicator of economic success, as figure 2.2 illustrates. Statistically the share of MSE employment tended to increase when economic growth was slow or negative, while the share decreased in years of strong economic growth.

---

[8] SMEDA (2002), based on data from the Survey of Household and Manufacturing Industries, 1987/88 and 1996/97.

[9] Results of the 2000 Census are not available at the time of writing.

Figure 2.2 Correlation between percentage GNP variations and MSE employment
proportions, Peru, 1986–2000

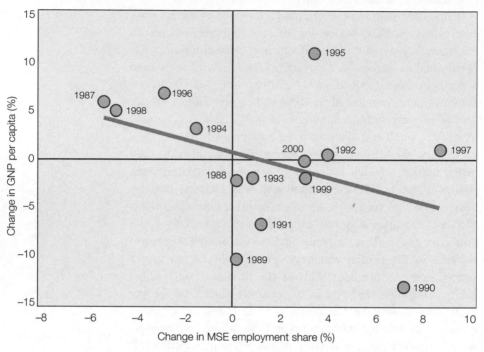

Source: Chacaltana (2001), using data from ENAHO and from the Central Reserve Bank of Peru.

While reforms were successful in making the tax system in Peru more transparent, reducing the costs of compliance and bringing more MSEs into the tax net, the liberalization of labour laws has not had such positive results. In fact, although it is much easier now to comply with labour regulation than at the beginning of the 1990s, the share of employees without written work contracts has increased, and most of this increase is concentrated in MSEs.

MSEs in Chile   The final category of countries investigated contains only Chile, where drastic economic liberalization took place during the 1970s and 1980s. During the 1990s, some significant additional reforms toward liberalization were made (particularly in the field of trade and finance policies), but most policy efforts were focused on ensuring continued growth and alleviating some of the social costs of the earlier reforms. Chile is the only country where the MSE share in non-agricultural employment declined over the 1990s.

There is no direct evidence on the evolution of employment shares by enterprise size class during the abrupt market reforms before 1990. However, the number of self-employed workers and small enterprises increased during this period, while at the same time economic wealth concentrated in conglomerates of large enterprises. According to national labour force surveys, there were 55 employees per employer in the Chilean labour market in 1970. By 1986, this figure had dropped to 20 (Reinecke, 2000, table 3.10).

While it was the declared objective of the market reforms in Chile to open up new opportunities for private enterprises, there was no special attention paid to the concerns of MSEs, many of which were established in response to the extremely high unemployment rates during economic recessions in the late 1970s and early 1980s. Between 1992 and 2002, the share of micro-enterprises in non-agricultural employment in Chile decreased slightly from 46.7 to 45.3 per cent. During the period of fast economic growth, 1992–97, micro-enterprises tended to reduce their employment share, while the recession in 1998 and 1999 led to an increase. However, many MSEs that survived the crisis are still struggling with the financial consequences which hamper their sustainability and employment creation potential. Over the 1992–2002 period, statistically the share of enterprises with one to four workers in non-agricultural employment tended to decrease in years of fast economic growth, but increased when economic growth was slow or negative.[10]

Each of the countries under study has something to tell us about the influence that policies have on MSE employment. In the first instance, they show how the pattern of MSE employment is linked to macroeconomic policy shifts. Both liberalization policies and the downsizing of the public sector contributed to increases in the MSE employment share.

The country cases also illustrate how the net contribution of MSE establishment and expansion in developing countries varies depending on the macroeconomic conditions. Both in Peru and in Chile, the MSE employment share tended to

---

[10] Authors' analysis based on data from the Instituto Nacional de Estadística (Encuesta Nacional de Empleo, October–December of each year) and the Central Bank of Chile (GDP in constant prices, fourth quarter of each year).

increase when GDP growth was slow or negative, whereas it decreased in times of economic boom. In Chile, we could identify this countercyclical pattern particularly among the smallest enterprises, suggesting a "buffer" function within the labour market.

More generally, in times of rapid economic growth, existing MSEs expand as entrepreneurs identify and respond to market opportunities. This creates a significant number of new jobs, and the incomes obtained through such activity are typically high and often rise. In contrast, in times of recession or crisis, the number of existing MSEs tends to contract; at the same time, new enterprises are likely to be started up, but these are often in activities that yield only low returns (Mead, 1994, p. 1882; Mead and Liedholm, 1998, p. 69).

MSEs often have to compensate employment losses elsewhere

Unfortunately, the macroeconomic policy shifts that have contributed to MSE growth in most countries have not necessarily produced a better labour market situation. In most cases, increased MSE employment has been accompanied by a decline in employment in the public sector and in large enterprises. Thus, in many cases, especially South Africa and the United Republic of Tanzania, the establishment of micro-enterprises appears to be a response by unemployed people who are moving into the MSE sector to create their own employment. In the context of public sector downsizing and the shrinking of larger enterprises, MSE employment is often a last resort to earn a livelihood. In South Africa and the United Republic of Tanzania, around one-third of the MSE owner-managers surveyed for this study gave as their main reason for managing an MSE "previous employment ended" or "cannot find other work". This share was somewhat lower in other countries, especially in Viet Nam, where a minority of only 13 per cent gave one of these reasons for being in business. In most countries, the share of owner-managers in business for negative reasons was higher among the micro-enterprises than among small enterprises.

From this evidence it can be determined that governments have increased the volume of employment in the MSE sector in two main ways. The most common channel has been the liberalization of their economies and the creation of macro-economic reforms that have offered new market opportunities to MSEs. While not always associated with national economic growth, MSEs have found niche markets and opportunities in these newly liberalized economies that were not previously there. This is particularly the case in Viet Nam, as the shift from a command economy to a more market-oriented economy has given rise to new private sector activity, and in South Africa, where the majority of the population now released from the exclusionary confines of apartheid are now able to participate more fully in the economy.

The second way governments have increased the volume of employment in the MSE sector is associated with the first, but is less direct. As governments have pursued programmes of economic reform, they have shed jobs in other sectors. Public sector reform, for example, caused a decline in public sector employment in many countries, while restructuring of state-owned enterprises in countries such as Viet Nam and the United Republic of Tanzania has also led to lay-offs. This has increased the already substantial pool of unemployed. Thus, with increasing competition for jobs, many unemployed women and men are forced to consider the prospects of employment in MSEs. Inadvertently, and while pursuing other economic outcomes (such as improvements in the efficiency of the public sector), these policies have contributed to growth in the volume of employment in the MSE sector.

It can be seen from the above analysis that the growth of MSE employment is not attributable to successful economic or social policies, but rather to policy biases, gaps and inconsistencies. This has contributed to an MSE sector that, while substantially larger than any other enterprise sector in employment terms, has been forced to operate informally and which experiences severe disadvantages in its capacity to participate fully in the economy, increase productivity levels and provide quality jobs.

The primary gap in the policy framework that we have identified is the lack of explicit attention paid by governments to the MSE sector. As we have seen from our brief outline of the economies of our sample countries, employment in MSEs has grown despite this gap and mainly as a result of broader government initiatives. The MSE sector and its workers have increased through a kind of trickle-down process in which the outcomes of macro-policy change have indirectly influenced the volume of employment in this sector. Governments have

Governments often treat employment and MSEs as residuals of economic policy

treated employment as a "residual" when carrying out reforms of economic policies, the assumption being that employment growth would follow automatically once sound finance, budgetary and trade policies were in place.

The results of this policy gap are well illustrated by the impact it has on women. Women are worse off than men: they are usually over-represented among the unemployed and, as we have seen, more prevalent in micro-enterprises than in small enterprises. Although there is little evidence to show that this is a direct result of either positive or negative bias in policies and laws, we do know that often those laws prohibiting the discrimination of women are not properly implemented. The high representation of women in micro-enterprises appears to be a result of this higher number of unemployed women, who, with additional family and household responsibilities, then enter the MSE sector for survival reasons. In general, cultural and social factors have a strong influence on this situation, but the lack of government attention given to the MSE sector increases the vulnerability of women working in it.

Despite the crucial importance of MSEs for the labour market and the economy in developing countries, many policies, laws and regulations are still designed with a view to large enterprises' needs only, while MSEs are not taken into account. Policies that cannot be applied to MSEs miss the large majority of enterprises and employment. Such policies are therefore unlikely to attain their goals for economic and social development.

2.2 Job quality in MSEs: A policy challenge

Job quality has a crucial influence on workers' well-being and poverty reduction

The national policy framework's influence on the growth in the volume of employment in MSEs tells only part of the story. The other dimension to MSE employment is found in its qualitative aspects. The term "job quality" refers to a range of employment-related factors that have an influence in the economic, social and psychological well-being of workers. It includes fundamental human rights at work, as identified by the International Labour Conference in its 1998 Declaration on Fundamental Principles and Rights at Work and its follow-up, as well as other dimensions of work.

There are a number of features of job quality in MSEs that can be assessed. Where relevant data can be found, the job quality can be measured by considering three broad fields. First, there are job quality issues that stem from the contractual arrangements between MSE owner-managers and their workers. These include issues such as remuneration levels (level of earnings, fringe benefits, non-wage benefits, hours of work), job security (the use of employment contracts, length of tenure), social protection (provision of health, life, disability and unemployment insurance, pension schemes, childcare, maternity benefits), freedom of association (the right to form trade unions) and freely chosen employment (absence of bonded labour, exploitative apprenticeship arrangements).

There are also job quality issues that concern the environment in which workers are located. These include the prevention of occupational accidents and diseases, the containment of environmental hazards and the promotion of health in the workplace. Physical working conditions can also be assessed by the amount of space provided for workers, eating facilities and sanitary installations that take account of the needs of women and men respectively.

Finally, there are job quality issues concerning investments into worker productivity and advancement. These include human resource development (provision of education and training opportunities, prospects of promotion and incentives for improvement) and management and organization arrangements (industrial relations practices and employee representation or participation in management).

The challenge of improving job quality in MSEs is directly linked to that of poverty eradication. Work hazards leave many people in developing countries poor because their ruined health no longer allows them to work; lack of social protection in the case of illness or retirement may push workers into poverty; and incomes in many MSEs can simply be too low to enable workers to live above the poverty line.

The quality of national data on employment quality in MSEs varies across the seven countries, such that close cross-country analysis within our sample is not possible. However, available data show that in all seven countries, the quality of employment in MSEs was lower than that in larger enterprises. In Guinea and the United Republic of Tanzania, public sector

MSE employment is of lower quality than employment in larger enterprises

33

workers receive salaries below the mean for MSE workers, but they have other benefits that MSE workers do not have. On average, there is no doubt that the smaller the enterprise, the lower the quality of employment.

The example of Tanzanian manufacturing enterprises illustrates well the differences in job quality between size classes, as presented in table 2.3. Compared to large enterprises, MSEs pay lower wages to production workers even though workers in MSEs have longer working hours. MSEs are also less likely than large enterprises to grant overtime pay, paid leave, or food or housing allowances. The coverage of social protection, the rate of unionization and the indicators for training activities are also lower among MSEs. Enterprise surveys in South Africa also show that the likelihood of formal training, as well as the rates of unionization and collective bargaining, increase with the size of the firm (Chandra et al., 2001a, 2001b).

Peruvian and Chilean labour force survey data also allow us to compare aspects of job quality by size of enterprise, as summarized in table 2.4, and the same trends can be perceived. Workers in MSEs in both countries receive substantially lower salaries than workers in larger enterprises. In Peru, a small part of this income gap can be attributed to the longer average working hours for workers in large enterprises; however, this difference in working hours is far less important than the gap in income. The coverage of pension schemes and health insurance is also much lower in MSEs than in larger enterprises, even though in Chile micro-enterprise workers are better covered than in Peru. Moreover, workers in MSEs are less likely to have written work contracts and to access training programmes than their colleagues in larger enterprises. Finally, workers in MSEs have a higher risk of suffering work accidents. In Chile, the rate of accidents is more than twice as high in micro-enterprises with one to ten workers than in large enterprises with more than 500 workers (Dirección del Trabajo, 2000b, p. 13).

These findings on job quality are in line with previous studies, most of which focus on wages. On average, jobs in small enterprises are less productive and less remunerated than jobs in larger enterprises, even after controlling for observable worker characteristics, such as education, sex and age (Steel and Takagi, 1983; Berry and Mazumdar, 1991; Schaffner, 1998;

Table 2.3   Job quality indicators in manufacturing firms by enterprise size, United
Republic of Tanzania, 1993 (percentages)

	Micro	Small	Medium	Large
Remuneration of production workers				
Wage (large enterprises =100)	79.7	68.9	96.8	100.0
Average weekly working hours	51	46	45	44
Enterprises paying benefits to production workers				
Food allowances	18	48	60	88
Housing allowances	18	49	70	96
Enterprise paying overtime and paid leave				
Overtime pay	13	45	72	96
Paid leave	22	57	82	100
Unionized enterprises	12	35	64	96
Workers receiving training				
Inside the enterprise	1.5	5.1	2.6	7.3
Outside training	3.1	5.4	5.6	6.9
Enterprises paying social protection				
Health care	25	54	82	100
Health care for family	12	37	48	78
Sick leave	24	52	68	100
Pension fund	15	54	78	93

Note: The enterprise size classes are defined here as follows: micro-enterprises are enterprises with one to four employees, small enterprises employ between five to 25 employees, medium enterprises are enterprises with more than 25 but less than 100 employees, and large enterprises are enterprises employing 100 employees or more.

Source: Goedhuys (2002) based on the World Bank RPED (Regional Program on Enterprise Development) data set of approximately 200 formal and informal manufacturing enterprises.

Hughes, 1999; Oi and Idson, 1999; Söderbom and Teal, 2001).[11] The study by Söderbom and Teal (2001, pp. 9–10), for instance, estimates that in Ghana's manufacturing sector, a 10 per

---

[11] Some studies suggest however that the small/large enterprise gap is narrowing in some Organisation for Economic Co-operation and Development (OECD) countries (OECD, 1996, pp. 61–62).

Table 2.4   Job quality indicators by enterprise size, Peru and Chile, 2000

	Chile					Peru				
	Self-employed	Micro	Small	Medium and large	Total	Micro[1]	Small	Medium	Large	Total
Average earnings (total average earnings =100)[2]	92.1	98.5	99.8	110.3	100.0	75.6	142.7	234.6	295.2	100.0
Hours worked per week	51.0	50.5	50.5	50.6	51.1	42.0	43.6	51.5	49.8	42.9
Health insurance (% of employment)	77.4	85.2	93.4	96.0	88.4	9.8	32.6	66.1	77.1	18.8
Pension (% of employment)	24.9	58.3	82.3	90.4	65.5	4.6	30.8	66.0	74.9	14.2
Written contract[3] (% waged employment)	...	61.2	83.2	90.6	77.7	24.8	59.2	87.9	85.4	..
Training[4]	4.2	8.0	17.2	30.4	16.4	31.2	44.1	58.0		42.5

Notes: The enterprise size classes are defined as follows: micro-enterprises are enterprises with two to nine persons (including the owner-manager), small enterprises employ between 10 and 49 persons, medium enterprises are enterprises with more than 50 but fewer than 200 workers, and large enterprises are enterprises employing 200 persons or more. Data for Peru are based on ENAHO 2000 and exclude only the public sector.

.. not available; ... not applicable. [1] Includes self-employment except for data on written contract and training. [2] Data refer to 1998 for Chile. [3] Data for Peru are from 1999 and refers to Metropolitan Lima only. [4] Data for Chile and Peru refer to different questions. In Chile the question asked was: "Have you received work-related training of any kind during the last 12 months?" Data for Peru cover only urban Peru and correspond to the share of private paid workers who have received or are receiving some type of training.

cent rise in enterprise size is statistically associated with a 1.6 per cent rise in earnings.

For many MSE workers, incomes are not sufficient for their households to leave poverty behind. In Chile, for example, 13 per cent of the workers in micro-enterprises (excluding self-employed workers) lived in poverty in 1998, while this share was considerably lower among large enterprise workers (7 per cent). According to a study of 14 Latin American countries (Orlando and Pollack, 2000), the incidence of poverty during the 1990s was about twice as high for workers in micro-enterprises than for workers in larger enterprises. However, employers in micro-enterprises on average earn more than employees in large enterprises. Thus, poor workers can move out of poverty by setting up their own micro-enterprises.

Table 2.5   Gender gap in incomes (male/female averages) by enterprise size,
Chile and Peru, 2000

	Self-employed (1 worker)	Other micro-enterprises (2 to 9 workers)	Small enterprises (10 to 49 workers)	Medium enterprises (50 to 199 workers)	Large enterprises (200 and more workers)
Chile	2.0	1.8	1.8	1.4	
Peru	2.0		1.4	1.4	1.3

Sources: Flores (forthcoming) and Chacaltana (2001).

For women, average job quality is even poorer than for men. It is not entirely clear whether this gender gap across our sample MSEs is wider or narrower than that in larger enterprises, but in the cases of Chile and Peru, the research results show the differences to be wider in MSEs, as table 2.5 illustrates. On the other hand, the gap in social security coverage in Peru seems to be narrower among MSE workers than among workers of larger enterprises. *The gender gap in MSE job quality*

However, another study taking into account the number of hours worked brings different results. An ILO study of 15 Latin American countries found that the gender gap in micro-enterprises was narrower than in larger enterprises (ILO, 2001a). Average hourly incomes of female employees in enterprises with up to five workers are 97 per cent of the average for male employees. In enterprises with more than five workers, women only earn 88 per cent of what men earn.

Improving job quality in MSEs and narrowing the job quality gap between MSEs and larger enterprises is not only a direct contribution to poverty eradication; it also increases enterprise productivity and profits. Table 2.6 presents information on the share of the sample MSEs across the seven countries that provided various types of benefits to their workers, and the owner-manager's perception on the enterprise's performance. The majority of MSEs that provided a benefit reported its positive impact on enterprise performance. This was also the case for benefits that are too often perceived merely as costs for the entrepreneur – such as written employment contracts and pension schemes. It can be concluded that improving job quality is a key to protecting MSE workers from poverty and to making MSEs more profitable. *Improving job quality makes enterprises more productive and profitable*

Table 2.6 Surveyed MSEs across the seven countries offering benefits to their workers, and rate of success (percentages)

Benefits	Enterprises offering benefit	Enterprises (of those that offer benefit) reporting better performance as a consequence
On-the-job training	47.9	91.4
Off-the-job training	15.1	85.6
Written employment contracts	25.5	61.1
Pension or old age insurance scheme	19.2	55.8
Health and accident insurance	26.8	56.1
Parental leave	24.6	59.9
Productivity incentives	45.3	86.4
Salary increase	41.4	82.2
Safer working conditions	45.5	75.5

Source: Christensen and Goedhuys (forthcoming) based on ILO MSE Surveys 2001.

The job quality gap between small and large depends on policies

The finding that job quality is lower in MSEs than in larger enterprises may appear obvious at first sight. However, what is interesting is that where time-trend data exist, the gap has increased over the 1990s.[12] Moreover, this gap in job quality persists not by chance but due to policy neglect or unintended consequences of policies. Regulations that make it extremely difficult for MSEs to comply or which are biased against MSEs contribute to the gap.

Economic liberalization and shifts in the macroeconomic development strategy alone are not enough to improve the situation of MSE workers. More specific policies and laws are needed to improve the quality of MSE employment, and those that exist need to be modified to improve both their coverage and the facility of compliance.

2.3 Policies and markets: Twin impact on small enterprises

The most important of the possible links that connect the national policy framework and MSE owner-managers is the market. It is

---

[12] This is the case in Chile and Peru. In the other countries under study, the measurement of employment quality over time was not possible due to lack of statistical information.

easy to see markets as separate from the realms of government, especially in the predominant free-market approach of our times. Governments are encouraged not to tamper with markets and to allow them to do what they do best: allocate resources as efficiently as possible. However, whether they are "free" or not, markets can only operate within a policy and legal environment that is shaped by social norms, governments and public law. It is this environment in which MSE owner-managers take decisions about the size of their workforce and the quality of employment they offer their employees.

One of the objectives of our study has been to find out which factors influence the employment decisions taken by MSE owner-managers, such as whether to hire additional staff, maintain current staffing levels or perhaps reduce the workforce. We were interested to find out whether decisions to change or maintain a certain employment level in the enterprise came from factors that were internal to the enterprise (for example, managing limited resources, restructuring, changing motivations) or whether they were the result of external influences. To address this issue we commissioned the MSE surveys, which investigated the significance of a range of possible influences: the cost of employment, labour regulations, access to finance and other resources, the market, the business premises, export, taxation, and government laws and policies.

The information on perceived factors of influence is inevitably subjective and has therefore to be interpreted with caution. However, even MSE owner-managers' perceptions that are based on incomplete or biased information are likely to have an impact on their actual decisions and therefore constitute relevant information. Across all seven countries, MSE owner-managers cited market forces as the most influential factor in their employment decisions from 1999 to 2001. This was found among both women and men, regardless of their qualifications and the characteristics of their enterprise.

MSE owner-managers perceive markets as a key factor in employment decisions

We also wanted to know which influences are perceived as "positive", that is, factors that encourage owner-managers to employ more staff. The survey results for this are shown in table 2.7. Across all countries, owner-managers perceived the market (demand for their products and services) as the main influence on positive employment decisions, followed by the availability of business premises (space for more staff). At first

Table 2.7   Factors positively influencing employment decisions in surveyed MSEs
            (mentions in percentages)

	Chile	Guinea	Pakistan	Peru	South Africa	Tanzania, United Rep. of	Viet Nam
The market	24.0	52.9	57.4	29.8	72.0	52.7	85.9
Business premises	11.7	32.1	44.1	17.2	53.8	26.7	36.9
Cost of employment	17.0	19.9	30.6	10.4	31.9	9.7	26.0
Labour regulations	1.3	12.8	19.8	7.6	18.6	5.3	7.1
Access to finance	8.0	14.7	33.0	7.3	30.5	18.0	26.6
Access to resources	8.0	26.6	30.0	10.1	28.0	20.0	17.9
Export	1.3	7.4	14.7	3.1	2.5	3.3	5.4
Taxation	3.0	5.4	18.0	7.0	14.7	2.0	14.1
Government policies	5.3	8.7	17.4	4.4	11.5	3.0	12.2

Source: ILO MSE Surveys 2001.

sight, MSE owner-managers in all seven countries perceive the influence of market changes much more strongly than other factors. The market was mentioned as a positive influencing factor at the highest rate in Viet Nam, at 85.9 per cent, where the economy has been growing, and lowest in Chile and Peru, at 24 and 29.8 per cent, where an economic slowdown occurred between 1999 and 2001. However, even in Chile, the influence of the market factor is assessed more positively than the influence of other factors.

By contrast, labour costs, labour regulation, government policies and taxation are the factors be perceived, on average, as least conducive to employment creation (Christensen and Goedhuys, forthcoming). This finding was valid for the sample as a whole and for some individual countries, such as Pakistan, Peru, the United Republic of Tanzania and Viet Nam. Some differences stand out, however. Labour regulation and taxation are seen as comparatively favourable factors in South Africa and Chile (labour regulation less so in Chile), while in Guinea and South Africa it is access to finance that is perceived as a constraining factor. These findings are consistent with the taxation systems in these countries. Where it is complex (Guinea and Pakistan) or involves numerous taxes (the United Republic of Tanzania), the system is perceived as highly constraining. Where tax systems are more

Table 2.8   Perceived influence of government policies on employment decisions in surveyed MSEs (percentages)

		Chile	Guinea	Pakistan	Peru	South Africa	Tanzania, United Rep. of	Viet Nam
Positive influence	Micro	2.5	8.1	10.1	3.3	9.2	3.5	7.5
	Small	8.6	11.5	25.0	9.2	30.0	2.0	20.4
No influence	Micro	51.6	69.6	60.9	58.7	60.2	57.7	88.9
	Small	54.7	69.2	36.0	55.1	50.0	56.6	77.9
Negative influence	Micro	46.0	22.3	29.0	38.3	30.5	35.3	3.5
	Small	36.7	19.2	39.0	35.7	20.0	37.4	1.8

Source: ILO MSE Surveys 2001.

transparent (Chile) or enforcement less stringent (South Africa), the perception is less negative. This analysis is continued in more detail in Chapter 4.

When examining the influence of government policies on employment decisions, we found that in most countries MSE owner-managers did not believe that government policies played a role in their decisions, as table 2.8 illustrates.[13] Only in Pakistan, South Africa and Viet Nam did a relatively high share of entreprneurs see government policies as having a positive influence on employment. However, given that the influence of policies can often be indirect, it may be invisible to MSE owner-managers.

In general, small enterprise owner-managers were found to believe that government policies had a positive influence at a higher rate than micro-entrepreneurs; this rate was highest in South Africa, followed by Pakistan and Viet Nam. The United Republic of Tanzania is the exception, where micro-enterprises were found to view government policies slightly more positively than small enterprises. Overall, it would seem that small enterprises see themselves as more influenced by government policies, both negatively and positively, whereas micro-enterprises sense little influence at all, perhaps explaining the correspondingly different levels of compliance with government laws and regulations between these groups. This

---

[13] In addition to the answer "government policies", the questionnaire also provided the separate answer options "labour regulations" and "taxation" (see table 2.7). Thus, the figures may underestimate the perceived direct influence of government policies.

issue will be taken up in the next chapter, where the decisions by enterprises to comply with laws and regulations are discussed.

Differences between growing and non-growing enterprises

Large and statistically significant differences in perception exist between enterprises that expanded employment between 1999 and 2001 and those that did not (Christensen and Goedhuys, forthcoming). In Peru, for example, the employment growth of enterprises seems to be driven by a favourable demand for products and the availability of good premises. Despite growth, the regulatory and policy environment is not perceived as conducive. Less successful enterprises seem to relate their stagnation to a lack of demand for their output and the regulatory and policy environment. In Chile, successful MSEs refer to markets, premises and inputs as engines for growth, while owner-managers of stagnating enterprises point to an unfavourable export market.[14] This is also true for growing enterprises, albeit to a lesser extent. Given the export orientation of Chile, enterprises may be sensitive to a downturn in export earnings, which affects entrepreneurs in their employment decisions. In Guinea, a lack of finance and the burden of taxation is keeping enterprises from expanding the workforce. For those enterprises that have overcome these constraints and have grown, their growth intensity may well be tempered by the tax burden. In the United Republic of Tanzania, successful entrepreneurs view their success as a result of market conditions and despite a constraining policy environment with high taxation, regulation and labour costs.

As shown at the beginning of this chapter, macroeconomic policies have influenced the pattern of MSE employment in all the countries studied. Macroeconomic policies that are market-oriented have been found to create new opportunities for the establishment and growth of MSEs. This view is supported by MSE owner-managers, who consistently claim that their decisions are mostly affected by changes in the market-place, and by the evidence that shows how policy gaps, inconsistencies and biases have contributed to creating inferior conditions of employment in the MSE sector and weaken the sector as a whole.

---

[14] The importance of export markets for MSEs is surprising, as a huge majority of MSEs serve only domestic markets. However, some of these may export indirectly, by providing inputs to export enterprises.

When they work well, markets can enhance the performance of MSEs by providing an environment in which enterprise owner-managers can make clear decisions regarding employment, investments or any other business management topics. Markets can provide an efficient means through which commercial transactions take place. However, markets can falter. They can exclude certain participants, or favour some over others. They can also work inefficiently and thus disadvantage many who work in them. They can lock MSEs into unrewarding activities, create bottlenecks and sometimes facilitate outright exploitation (Albu and Scott, 2001). Just as sound market-oriented macroeconomic policies can broaden the market base in which MSEs operate, adjustments to the policy and legal environment can facilitate the development of markets. Governments and market institutions are key players in these adjustments.

Influencing the market to make it more effective

Economist Douglas North describes institutions as "the humanly-devised constraints that structure human interaction. They are composed of formal rules (statute law, common law, regulations), informal constraints (conventions, norms of behaviour, and self imposed codes of conduct), and the enforcement characteristics of both" (North, 1994, p. 1). He distinguishes institutions from organizations. Organizations also specify the constraints that structure human interaction, but in addition they are action groups.

> They are composed of groups of individuals bound by a common purpose to achieve objectives. They include political bodies (political parties, the senate, a city council, a regulatory agency); economic bodies (firms, trade unions, family farms, cooperatives); social bodies (churches, clubs, athletic associations); and educational bodies (schools, colleges, vocational training centers). Organizations in pursuit of their objectives are the primary source of institutional change. (North, 1994, p. 2)

Organizations perform within an institutional framework. Together, institutions and organizations thus have an important role in building and shaping markets (World Bank, 2002). Policies can affect markets by determining the legal and regulatory parameters under which enterprises operate, and they can influence the role of the institutions, which in turn can affect which policies are adopted.

Governments also have an important role to play in the market. In most instances, market transactions depend on the development of a third party to exchanges, namely government,

Markets for MSEs are linked to the policy environment

which specifies property rights and enforces contracts, and on the existence of norms of behaviour to constrain parties in interaction (North, 1989). Governments can thus facilitate the role that markets perform in the allocation of resources as well as in the decision-making processes of MSE owner-managers.

The ways in which markets can affect the performance of MSEs are interrelated, and can provide different perspectives on the operations of the market, the link between the market and the policy environment, and the role of governments and institutions.[15] The first way markets can affect the performance of MSEs is through the enabling framework – the policy, legal and regulatory framework in which markets operate. At its broadest level, the enabling framework is affected by the macroeconomic strategy of the country and the extent that it promotes market functions. It also includes the political and social culture in which markets operate and the prevailing systems of governance. Good governance provides a sound administrative basis for market transactions that require consistency and predictability.

The enabling framework for market activities is also affected by the legal and administrative systems that govern its operations. Economic courts, the application of commercial standards and the rule of law are examples of legal and administrative systems that can improve the operations of the market. There are many examples to be found where legal and administrative systems fail to meet the needs of MSEs. For example, there can be situations where the costs of establishing and enforcing agreements (transaction costs) are so high that markets cannot operate effectively for MSEs. Moreover, policy decisions can directly affect the access of MSEs to specific markets, for instance in tendering for public sector infrastructure projects (box 2.1).

Finally, the enabling framework also includes the regulation of market protocols. These may be derived locally, nationally or internationally. Local, national or international restrictions on trade, for example, can reduce the effectiveness of the market and constrain its capacity to promote more and better jobs.

Markets can exclude MSEs

The second way markets can affect the performance of MSEs is through the presence of adverse power relations and

---

[15] Adapted from United Kingdom Department for International Development (2000).

Box 2.1   Policies and employment-intensive investment: A market for small
           enterprises

Government policies have a crucial role in giving small enterprises a fair chance to explore
new markets. For example, SMEs can work as contractors for public work projects at lower
cost than large-scale enterprises while creating more employment opportunities. Yet, in many
countries, SMEs face enormous obstacles in obtaining public contracts. Tenders are often
designed for large enterprises, and the tendering system may not be transparent.

While for some large-scale infrastructure projects, such as energy, telecommunications or
airports, labour-based methods are no alternative to equipment-intensive technology,
new markets can be opened up for SMEs in the construction of feeder roads, minor dams
and social infrastructure. This requires political will and a strengthened technical and
managerial capacity of the public sector. Contract specifications need to be adjusted to
give priority to light instead of heavy equipment. The contractual system also includes the
division of public tenders into small contracts that are accessible to SMEs.

Comparative studies carried out by the ILO in various developing countries show that,
without compromising the quality of the infrastructure, the labour-based option:

- is between 10 and 30 per cent less costly than more equipment-intensive options;
- reduces foreign exchange requirements by some 50 to 60 per cent; and
- creates between two and four times more employment for the same investment.

A small contractor development project in Ghana provided comprehensive training on
labour-based works to SME staff as well as to Government engineers and supervisors.
Between 1989 and 1996, over 1,500 km of roads were built and 3,500 km were
rehabilitated, creating some 4.4 million work-days of temporary employment. At an
average wage of approximately US$1 per day, some US$4.4 million was injected into
rural economies as direct cash wages. Substantial indirect spin-offs in terms of
employment creation were obtained through investments in housing improvements, local
production of hand tools, farm rehabilitation and social expenditure.

Source: ILO Employment-Intensive Investment Programme.

market exclusions. This refers to the impact that imbalances in
power relationships can have on the operation of the market,
especially where certain groups (for example, MSEs and
women) are excluded from full and equal participation in the
market. This can result from laws, regulations or institutions
that are biased. Such exclusions or imbalances can also result
from social relations established through custom, such as

bonded labour situations or traditional relations that prevent women from owning or inheriting property.

Adverse power relations can contribute to distortions in market power and economies of scale, creating barriers to entry, enabling monopoly rents to be earned and depressing production. They can also lead to asymmetric information – imbalances in the kinds and quality of information held by different parties to a transaction about the nature of the exchange. Each of these practices excludes participants from the market and reduces the effectiveness of the market.

Moreover, links between different markets can contribute to exclusion. Vulnerability or disadvantage in one market system (such as financial markets) can create or contribute to vulnerability or disadvantage in another market system (such as labour markets).

Many MSEs find entry into the market-place easy, especially those operating in the informal economy. However, the informal economy often excludes its participants from the legal and regulatory mechanisms that can protect them. An enabling legal, policy and regulatory environment should allow markets to operate effectively and should facilitate participation. MSEs in the informal economy in Peru, for example, were found to believe that their lack of access to markets was the major disadvantage of operating outside of the regulatory framework (Robles et al., 2001, pp. 180–181).

Redressing imbalances in power relationships in the market can broaden the participation of all groups and, hence, the competitiveness and effective of the market. This may involve reforming those laws and regulations that are biased against small enterprises or groups of small enterprises (such as women-owned enterprises) at national, provincial and local levels. It may also require a broader strategy to reform social relations that perpetuate exploitative, unfair or inequitable practices.

Market development initiatives should ensure that linkages between markets and the social and political structures and processes in which they operate do not exclude or disadvantage certain groups. This may require new schemes that help MSE owner-managers manage risk and reduce their vulnerability (such as local-based social security schemes). It may also involve processes that seek to identify and remove or reduce market linkages that spread vulnerability or disadvantage.

In sum, the policy and regulatory environment is crucial for the creation of decent employment in MSEs. The influence is both direct and indirect, via its impact on the market and the broader business environment. The following chapter discusses in detail how the design and implementation of laws and regulations can leverage more MSEs into the formal economy and strengthen their potential to create decent employment. Because jobs in MSEs are of poorer quality than those in larger enterprises, macroeconomic policies should be complemented with other more specific policy instruments that enhance the capacity of MSEs to improve the quality of the employment they offer. This will not only help workers to move out of poverty; it can also contribute to raising enterprises' productivity and economic development at large (ILO, 2002c).

The policy and legal environment is crucial for the creation of decent employment in MSEs

The findings presented in this chapter make plain the choice that policy-makers have when faced with employment concerns in their country. While employment creation is generally seen as a natural result of economic growth, this does not mean that it should be left alone. There is a tendency to intervene in employment only when it concerns labour regulation, which is usually the domain of labour ministries. To do this, however, ignores the forces that lead people into and out of certain kinds of employment.

We have seen that MSEs are the major employers in all seven countries studied and, indeed, this is a phenomenon that is witnessed around the world. We have also seen that this situation has not necessarily come about because of specifically designed policies to promote employment in the MSE sector, but has been created by other government intentions. Thus, the MSE sector contains many people who have taken the initiative to enter this sector out of the lack of any other employment alternative and it is one in which many workers experience a poor quality of employment.

Faced with this situation, policy-makers can choose between two broad options. One option is to continue on the path described above, placing MSE employment as a last resort for those who are unemployed and treating the MSE sector as a reserve pool of labour that may be drawn upon when the next cycle of economic growth hits. The MSE sector is marginalized, in this option, from the mainstream of the

There are two main choices open to policy-makers

economy and from the macro-policy framework, of which MSE employment is simply a by-product.

The second option available to policy-makers is to improve the connections between the MSE sector and national economic and social development objectives, recognizing MSEs for the current and potential roles they can perform in the national economy and incorporating them into the national development strategy. Within this option, policies and laws would be framed to influence the decisions of MSE owner-managers, both women and men, in ways that enhance their contribution to employment, in both qualitative and quantitative terms, as well as to GDP.

In pursuing the second option, policy-makers would not heighten the importance of the MSE sector above any others – since MSEs should operate alongside large and medium-sized enterprises. Such direct, biased intervention in the market-place has been proven faulty and unsustainable. Instead, they would improve MSEs' access to resources and product markets and thereby enhance the role of markets as the primary source of information upon which MSE owner-managers make their decisions. They would consider employment as an important goal of policy, rather than a residual of other policy choices.

Following the objectives of the second option, policy-makers are required to go beyond the development of markets and to look specifically at the ways in which the policy and legal environment affects MSE employment. This requires a closer look at how MSEs comply with government regulations, as well as a more detailed investigation into any anti-MSE biases that can be found in the policies and laws that govern small enterprise operations. The results of our investigation into these issues are presented in Chapters 3 and 4, respectively.

COMPLIANCE: A PATH FROM THE MARGINS TO THE MAINSTREAM

3

Complying with regulations is an expensive undertaking for MSEs in most developing countries. Consequently, the legal and regulatory debate generally focuses on the financial cost of compliance and the other burdens that regulations represent for MSEs and their potential to create employment. Reducing the cost of compliance is one of the key objectives in reforming the policy environment. However, this is only one side of the coin. In fact, compliance with regulations often helps enterprises develop and create more employment. By focusing not only on their regulatory functions but also on their facilitating role, governments can use compliance with regulations as a development tool.

This chapter describes the dynamic between the marginality of MSEs in the economy and the motivation and ability of these MSEs to comply with state requirements. It follows two themes. The first concerns the ways in which MSEs respond to the formal requirements of the State. We look at the continuum of compliance and formality among MSEs, illustrating the strategic nature of the responses that MSE owner-managers have to the policy and legal environment in which they operate.

The second theme to be examined in this chapter concerns the nature of a "conducive environment" for MSE promotion. This environment uses compliance as a development tool. We examine the benefits of compliance alongside some of the ways in which the State can make its policies and laws more responsive to the needs, capacities and opportunities of small enterprises. Thus, by designing a policy and legal environment around an accurate understanding of the MSE sector,

Between marginality and compliance

compliance can be increased, while the enterprises themselves gain better access to resources and greater official recognition.

Since the first conceptualization of the informal economy in the early 1970s, there has been a substantial body of work on this subject. Economists such as de Soto (1989; 2000) have examined ways in which MSEs have devised informal or extra-legal mechanisms of doing business when the legal and regulatory framework is ill suited to their needs or capacities. These studies have illustrated the loss of productivity and revenue for the national economy resulting from poorly designed laws and regulations. Djankov et al. (2000) have made international comparisons of the administrative cost of registering an enterprise. A number of compelling arguments for the removal or improvement of prohibitive registration and licensing procedures have been established through the work of these authors.

The challenge of job quality However, the relationship between labour laws and regulations and the MSE sector has featured less in this work. The reduction or elimination of labour laws and regulations may initially appear to be a necessary step for a more conducive environment for MSE growth. However, the removal of labour standards for MSEs would lead to further deficits in the quality of employment in these enterprises and contribute to the erosion of a number of substantial social gains that have been won for workers in all sectors of the economy. Hence, the challenge for labour laws and regulations as they apply to the MSE sector is to find ways in which laws and regulations can be used to establish and maintain agreed-upon standards for workers, while helping MSE owner-managers to incorporate good labour practices in their management decisions. This includes reforms to lower the cost of complying with labour regulations.

3.1 Responses to the legal and regulatory environment

Most MSEs in developing countries are neither completely formal nor completely informal. Instead of a formal versus informal dichotomy we have found a continuum of compliance and formality among MSEs. This reflects a range of responses by owner-managers to the formal requirements of the State. Box 3.1 summarizes the definitions of informality and provides a brief update on some of the issues surrounding this concept.

Box 3.1   Defining informality

The term "informal sector" was first used by the British economist Keith Hart and spread in ILO reports on Kenya at the beginning of the 1970s. In general terms, the people working in the informal sector are independent, self-employed producers in urban areas, some of whom employ family members and some of whom hire non-family workers or apprentices.

Informal sector activities usually require little or no capital, provide low incomes and unstable employment, and frequently operate amid unsafe working conditions. Because the informal sector is heterogeneous in terms of its activities and occupations, studies use various terms, definitions and categorizations. Diverse terms used to describe this economy include: shadow, unofficial, third, underground, grey, hidden, counter and parallel (Thomas, 1992, Ch. 6).

The 15th Session of the International Conference of Labour Statisticians in 1993 adopted an establishment-based definition. According to this definition, the informal sector may be broadly characterized as consisting of units engaged in the production of goods or services, with the primary objective of generating employment and incomes to the persons concerned. These units typically operate at a low level of organization, with little or no division between labour and capital as factors of production, and on a small scale. Labour relations – where they exist – are based mostly on casual employment, kinship or personal and social relations rather than contractual arrangements with formal guarantees.

The informal sector was defined as comprising:

a) informal own-account enterprises, which are household enterprises owned and operated by own-account workers, either alone or in partnership with members of the same or other households, which may employ contributing family workers and employees on an occasional basis, but do not employ employees on a continuous basis; and

b) enterprises of informal employers, which, for operational purposes, may be defined, depending on national circumstances, in terms of one or more of the following criteria: (i) size of the unit below a specified level of employment (determined nationally); (ii) non-registration of the enterprise or its employees under specific forms of national legislation, such as factories or commercial acts, tax or social security laws.

In the discussions of the 90th Session of the International Labour Conference, 2002 (ILO, 2002b and 2000a), the "informal economy" has been preferred to the "informal sector", because the workers and enterprises in question do not fall within any one sector of economic activity, but cut across many sectors:

Cont./

Cont./

The term "informal economy" refers to all economic activities that are – in law or in practice – not covered or insufficiently covered by formal arrangements. Their activities are not included in the law, which means that they are operating outside the formal reach of the law; or they are not covered in practice, which means that – although they are operating within the formal reach of the law, the law is not applied or not enforced; or the law discourages compliance because it is inappropriate, burdensome, or imposes excessive costs. (ILO, 2002a)

This new definition recognizes informal employment relations in formal enterprises as part of the informal economy. According to this definition, the informal economy is even more dominant in the labour markets of developing countries than generally acknowledged. For example, it accounts for 93 per cent of total employment in India and 62 per cent of total employment in Mexico (ILO, 2002e).

The notion of "insufficiently covered" recognizes that formality and informality do not constitute a dichotomy, but a continuum. Enterprises can be formal according to some regulatory criteria, while they are informal according to others. This is the argument that we develop in this book to flesh out the idea of using compliance with regulations as a means of employment creation and development.

In most developing countries MSEs are found somewhere on a continuum that spans full compliance and complete non-compliance

Formalization – referring to a transition from complete non-compliance toward compliance – is not something an enterprise acquires once and for all. Rather, it is an evolutionary and continuing process in which MSE owner-managers determine whether or not they are able or willing to continue meeting their legal obligations (Maldonado et al., 1999). In fact, there are two broad types of regulations: there are regulations related to becoming legal, notably registration and licensing; then there are regulations related to remaining legal, notably taxation and labour obligations, but also health and safety regulations (Chen et al., 2002).

Obviously, these two types of regulations are connected. When MSE owner-managers decide to comply with the first type of regulations they do so in the knowledge that it will increase the pressures on them to comply with the second type. Conversely, a fear or lack of desire to comply with the obligations required to remain legal may lead to a decision not to register a business formally in the first place.

Some countries have chosen to establish a legal status that is specific to certain categories of MSEs, which falls between formal and informal and responds to the realities of many

MSEs. In Viet Nam, for example, a type of MSE known as the "household enterprise" was assigned a semi-formal status in 1992. This allows household enterprises the advantages of formal recognition by government authorities through simplified and cheaper registration and reporting procedures. However, this semi-official status does not offer the full advantages that come with complete formalization, such as the MSE's right to sign contracts. Thus, these household enterprises have their own legal status, albeit without enjoying the full status of formal small and medium-sized enterprises.

In most countries, however, semi-formality simply arises from partial compliance with laws and regulations (Maldonado et al., 1999; Robles et al., 2001). The results of the MSE surveys across the seven countries confirm that the majority of MSEs operate in a semi-formal manner. This situation is just as much a result of the policies, laws and regulations that governments establish and attempt to enforce, as it is of the strategic choices that MSE owner-managers are faced with.

While the details of registrations with government agencies in specific policy areas will be dealt with in Chapter 4, the following discussion gives an overview of the continuum of formality and informality, based on results from the MSE surveys presented in tables 3.1 and 3.2.

Registration with tax authorities was required in all the countries we studied, but, as table 3.2 shows, compliance with this requirement was found to vary. Compliance rates were highest in Chile and Peru at more than 80 per cent. With the exception of South Africa, rates among MSE owner-managers in other countries were close to 60 per cent.[1] In order to comply with business laws and regulations, in most countries a separate registration was required, in some cases at both national and local levels. Compliance with these requirements was generally lower than in the case of tax authorities. Registration with labour authorities was consistently low, remaining below one-third of the sample MSEs in all countries except Peru. However, compliance with labour laws clearly increases as the size of the enterprise increases. In some countries, enterprises were also registered with government agencies related to trade and industry.

---

[1] In some countries, such as Pakistan and Viet Nam, tax authorities require separate registrations for different types of taxes. The information in table 3.1 refers to business income tax authorities.

Table 3.1   Registration rates of surveyed MSEs by types of registration, 2001
(percentages)

		Tax authorities (business income tax)	Business registration			
			National authorities	Local authorities	Labour authorities	Authorities for trade and industry
Chile	Micro	85.1	67.1	78.3	...	...
	Small	90.6	80.6	84.9	...	...
	Total	87.7	73.3	81.3	...	...
Guinea	Micro	74.6	20.8	...	8.1	...
	Small	69.2	30.8	...	17.3	...
	Total	73.7	22.4	...	9.6	...
Pakistan[1]	Micro	45.6	...	...	3.6	4.1
	Small	70.7	...	...	23.8	19.5
	Total	58.0	...	...	13.5	11.7
Peru	Micro	82.8	...	79.5	34.2	...
	Small	99.5	...	96.9	93.9	...
	Total	86.5	...	83.3	47.3	...
South Africa	Micro	25.3	...	20.5	13.3	8.0
	Small	73.3	...	60.0	40.0	16.7
	Total	30.5	...	24.7	16.1	9.0
Tanzania, United Rep. of	Micro	62.2	...	86.1	16.4	16.9
	Small	81.8	...	94.9	62.6	28.3
	Total	68.7	...	89.0	31.7	20.7
Viet Nam[2]	Micro	51.3	24.6	53.8	7.5	5.5
	Small	80.5	56.6	42.5	5.3	9.7
	Total	61.9	36.2	49.7	6.7	7.1

Note: ... not applicable. [1] Authorities with trade and industry correspond to Export Promotion Bureau only. [2] Local authorities correspond to the People's Committee. Household enterprises, of which the majority are micro-enterprises, are obliged to register and obtain the necessary licences for their business with the district People's Committee Business Bureau. Other private enterprises have to register with the (national) Planning and Investment Services at provincial level. Registration with labour authorities (job creation fund) is optional.

Source: ILO MSE Surveys 2001.

Registration with these authorities is required for specific sectors only or for enterprises that directly import or export.

The number of registrations that are required for an MSE to operate legally varies across countries and across economic sectors. For example, depending on its activity, an enterprise may be

Table 3.2   Compliance with basic registration requirements by surveyed MSEs, 2001 (percentages)

		Not complying with any basic registration requirements	Complying with some but not all registration requirements	Complying with all basic registration requirements
Chile	Total	8.0	26.7	65.3
	Micro	8.1	34.8	57.1
	Small	7.9	17.3	74.8
Guinea	Total	22.8	72.4	4.8
	Micro	21.5	75.0	3.5
	Small	28.8	59.6	11.5
Pakistan	Total	35.7	58.3	6.0
	Micro	46.7	47.3	5.9
	Small	24.4	69.5	6.1
Peru	Total	10.0	49.0	41.1
	Micro	12.8	59.6	27.7
	Small	0.0	11.2	88.8
South Africa	Total	61.6	28.3	10.0
	Micro	66.7	25.7	7.6
	Small	20.0	50.0	30.0
Tanzania, United Rep. of	Total	2.7	50.0	47.3
	Micro	3.5	55.7	40.8
	Small	1.0	38.4	60.6
Viet Nam	Total	6.7	92.6	0.6
	Micro	9.5	89.4	1.0
	Small	1.8	98.2	0.0

Note: In Viet Nam, enterprises not registered with any government agency have not been included in the sample. See p. 165 of the Annex for more details.

Source: ILO MSE Surveys 2001

required to register with an Industrial Council, Liquor Board, Estate Agents' Board, or to apply for a special trading licence. In order to allow comparison across countries, however, the following analysis focuses on general business registrations only. For each country, the most important general registration requirements in the areas of business laws and regulations, taxation and labour have been identified (see table A.6 in the Annex). Table 3.2 presents the degree of compliance with these requirements in the seven countries, both as a group and by micro and small class sizes.

Even in this simplified analysis of general business registrations, it becomes clear that many MSEs in the country under study do register with one or more government agencies, but do not fulfil all legal requirements. This was the case of the majority of the micro-enterprises in the sample in Guinea, Pakistan, Peru, the United Republic of Tanzania and Viet Nam. In Chile, a majority of micro-enterprises complied with all identified basic registration requirements, while in South Africa the majority did not fulfil any of these requirements. The report on South Africa (Mollentz, 2002) suggests that this high rate of unregistered enterprises may be due to the weakness of the institutions that enforce registration requirements.

As expected, the compliance with registration requirements was higher for small enterprises than for micro-enterprises in all seven countries, with a majority in Chile, Peru and the United Republic of Tanzania complying with all basic registration requirements. Considering that registration does not always imply full compliance with government regulations, it is safe to state that most MSEs can be found somewhere between complete formality and complete informality.

In summary, most MSEs register with at least one government agency, but do not fulfil all legal requirements. The next section deals with the factors in the policy and legal environment that determine the degree of MSEs' compliance with regulations.

3.2 Promoting desired enterprise behaviours

The legal and regulatory environment can be used to influence the behaviour of MSE owner-managers in two ways. It can be used in the most conventional sense through the rule of law. Through enforcement of laws and regulations, enterprises are prevented from behaving in undesirable ways. This usually involves the threat of fines, imprisonment or confiscation of business assets. Thus, enterprises are obliged to operate within the law and regulations of the day.

Another, less conventional use of laws and regulations is to enable. Here government facilitates compliance – and, hence, MSE development – through the design and implementation of laws and regulations that ascribe rights and benefits to an enterprise. The registering of intellectual property, for example, provides a right over the use of that property and protects the owner against unlawful use of that property by others.

This two-pronged approach to influencing the behaviour of enterprise owner-managers can be extremely powerful. However, to work properly, laws and regulations must be designed in a manner that reflects social norms while responding to the experiences and capacities of the MSE sector. Unfortunately, most governments have adopted a one-sided approach to this issue, introducing laws and regulations that offer few benefits or rights to the enterprise or its owner. This has contributed significantly to the decisions taken by many MSE owner-managers against compliance.

The decision to comply with regulations or not is a strategic one, based on the advantages and disadvantages that compliance or non-compliance brings, as well as on the capacity to comply. We have subscribed to a rational choice model to explain how an enterprise owner-manager responds to the policy and legal environment, as described in box 3.2. *Compliance is based on MSEs' assessment of costs and benefits*

Not all laws and regulations affect enterprises in the same way. While they all have the potential to restrict the operations of enterprises in one way or another, the effect of these restrictions is not uniform. The removal of all forms of laws and regulations does not necessarily lead to a more conducive environment for MSE employment, because it can remove rights and restrict the potential for commercial transactions. In some cases, new or improved laws and regulations are required to create an environment that facilitates commercial transactions in an efficient, market-oriented manner. De Soto (2000, pp. 183–4), for example, describes the need to systematize laws and regulations, such as property rights, based on the formalization of social contracts, so that everyone in society knows where they stand and can participate in commercial transactions.

Labour legislation performs an important function in the protection of workers. It can restrict enterprise owner-managers from engaging in exploitative, discriminatory or unsafe employment practices. Thus, while it may be desirable to reduce the regulatory obligations on MSEs in some fields, this is often not true when it comes to the regulation of labour. The costs of compliance with labour regulations can be *Labour legislation protects workers*

Box 3.2   Applying rational choice models to compliance decisions

Rational choice models assume that actors are making rational decisions in situations of uncertainty. Actors assess the expected costs and benefits, and act consistently with their preferences. They vary in their discount rates (that is, how much they care and plan for the future) and in their capacities to assess the risk they face. They are uncertain about the effects of the actions they and others take; they cannot even be absolutely certain about the actions of others.

This view on the decision-making dynamic of MSE owner-managers is summarized by Kuchta-Helbing (2000, p. 25):

> The bottom line is that entrepreneurs do a cost/benefit analysis of why they should or should not comply with regulations. Often, they comply with some regulations and not with others. Typically those in the informal sector fall on a continuum between formality and informality. Moreover, if institutions are weak and offer few or poor services or benefits, entrepreneurs have no incentive to abide by regulations or to pay for their operational costs.

The choices of MSE owners-managers, as viewed within a rational choice model, have been particularly important in our investigation because they provide what Levi (1997) has described as "the micro-foundations of macro-processes and events". Thus, they provide us with insights into how MSE owner-managers respond to the national policy and legal environment, which can then be used as a tool to understand the combined impacts of policies and laws on employment within small enterprises.

The choice an enterprise owner-manager makes is usually constrained by one of two major external sources. The first is a lack of resources such as money or time. This may prevent an owner-manager from doing what she or he wants. The second source of constraint is institutional and organizational. Because institutions and organizations set rules, these rules limit the choices of owner-managers. Often enterprise owner-managers make strategic decisions based on their evaluation of the behaviour of others before making their own choice. The decision to comply with a government decree, for example, will be affected by their assessment of what others are likely to do.

lowered, however, by making their implementation more flexible among MSEs.

In some countries, the legal and regulatory environment has been designed to help MSEs cut costs at the expense of job quality and the long-term perspectives of the enterprise. Labour legislation in Pakistan, for example, has been designed so that it applies to enterprises with ten or more employees. While this initially appears to be a positive response to the needs of smaller enterprises by reducing their costs of compliance, it has the effect of dissuading owner-managers from expanding their business beyond the threshold of nine employees. Instead of employing more people in their business, these owner-managers will often begin another business or employ casual or informal labour, simply to avoid the costs labour legislation will bring when they reach the ten-worker threshold. This clearly demonstrates how the exclusion of MSEs from the broader policy and legal framework creates disincentives to growth and deficits in job quality that undermine the productive potential of the sector and keep it in the margins.

Labour issues have a particular character in the MSE sector. Unlike large enterprises, MSEs have flat organizational and management structures. Ownership of an MSE implies a high degree of day-to-day administration, management and production work. Indeed, this is one of the characteristics of MSEs – apart from their size alone – that sets them apart from larger enterprises and state-owned enterprises. Moreover, many employees in MSEs can be family members, relatives or close friends. Because employment practices within MSEs are not always dealt with through the management–worker relationships that typify most medium-sized and large enterprises, their labour relations have a unique and diffuse character.

Of course, there are costs incurred by MSEs when complying with regulations. Nevertheless, as we will show later, there are also costs that stem from the failure to comply. Registering a business can be an expensive and time-consuming exercise, as summarized in box 3.3. There can be direct and indirect costs to complying with enterprise laws and regulations. The direct costs include fees for registration, licences and permits. They can also include the regular payments that must be made when reporting or otherwise fulfilling legal and fiscal obligations. The indirect costs of compliance can involve a broader range of financial and non-financial items, including the time it takes to collect the forms, complete them, await approval and regularly report on progress. For those enterprises located in rural or semi-rural areas, indirect costs can include the time and funds required to travel to the nearest responsible government agency.

Excessive costs of compliance can lead enterprises into ignoring or evading regulations

Compliance is not a one-off expense but "a flow of costs" that affects the decisions of MSE owner-managers to register.

Box 3.3   The costs of registration

The cumulative impact of business laws and regulations can reduce the profitability of MSEs. A recent World Bank study measured the time and monetary cost in 75 countries for an enterprise in the capital city to register. The study only measured official costs and excluded bribes and bureaucratic delays:

> The number of procedures required to start up an enterprise varies from the low of two in Canada to the high of 20 in Bolivia, with the world average of around ten. The minimum official time for such start up varies from the low of two days to the high of 174 business days, assuming that there are no delays by either the applicant or the regulators, with the worldwide average of 63 business days. The official cost of following these procedures for a simple enterprise ranges from under 0.4 per cent of per capita GDP to over 2.6 times per capita GDP, with a worldwide average of 34 per cent of annual per capita income. For an entrepreneur, legal entry is extremely cumbersome, time-consuming, and expensive in most countries of the world. (Djankov et al., 2000, p. 4)

The study also found that countries with heavier regulation of entry have larger unofficial economies but no better quality of public or private goods. This strengthens the argument in favour of reducing the burden of business laws and regulations.

Once registered, enterprises are expected to pay fees and taxes on a regular basis. They are also required to report to various government agencies for administrative and statistical purposes. Such a multiplicity of reporting requirements can create unnecessary costs for MSEs when reporting formats and intervals are not harmonized across government agencies. Moreover, official recognition may lead to more inspections, more fees to be paid, and greater monitoring. Often these added encumbrances are placed on the enterprise without the enterprise owner-manager seeing any benefit in return.

Compliance costs are proportionally much higher for smaller enterprises than for larger ones because of the significant fixed-cost elements of regulatory compliance. In OECD countries, micro- and small enterprises with one to 19 employees spent US$4,600 per employee per year, more than five times as much as enterprises with 50 to 500 employees. Moreover, while medium-sized and large enterprises usually have the scale and financial resources to employ administrative specialists or external experts, smaller enterprises are often forced to involve owner-managers in the detail of ensuring compliance with regulations. This affects the focus of business management (OECD, 2001). Hence, the high costs of compliance favour larger enterprises over small ones, even though the policy and legal environment may not be explicitly biased one way or the other.

In Chile and Peru, the registration system is generally more effective than in the other countries we studied, making it easier for an MSE owner-manager to register and thus enter the formal economy. In Viet Nam, on the other hand, the presence of People's Committees at the district and communal level throughout the country and the location of business bureaus within these encourage MSE owner-managers to register. Thus, there seems to be a clear correlation between required licences and a registration and monitoring system that encourages owner-managers to register on the one hand, and the rates of registration on the other.

According to the MSE surveys, in Chile the time needed for compliance was more problematic than the financial cost involved in registering with government and tax authorities. In the United Republic of Tanzania, on the contrary, the financial cost of registering with the tax authorities and with the employment fund was more problematic than the time involved in compliance, according to the sample MSEs unregistered with these authorities.

Non-compliance with laws and regulations has its cost too. *The cost of* This cost of non-compliance also features in the decision- *non-compliance* making process of MSE owner-managers. Non-compliance can attract police harassment and the potential of penalties that act as a disincentive to remaining informal. De Soto claims, for example, that the cost of doing business in Peru is higher for extra-legal enterprises because they are required to pay an average of 10 to 15 per cent of their annual income in bribes and commissions to authorities (De Soto, 2000, p. 85).

Beyond the illegal and unofficial costs of bribery and corruption, there are usually official enforcement mechanisms that serve to punish those who fail to comply. However, in many cases MSE owner-managers decide against compliance because the enforcing institutions are so weak and the informal economy so large that the chances of government penalties are slim. Indeed, the chances and costs of penalties such as fines may be less than the costs of compliance itself – especially when there are so many different institutions for which registration or some other form of compliance is required.

Benefits to MSEs through compliance can be hidden or intangible

The potential benefits arising from regulatory compliance are often neglected in analysis. In some countries the prevailing social and legal culture makes compliance a value in itself. In Chile, the fact that various registrations are a legal responsibility was the most-mentioned reason for registering with various government agencies. Similarly, in Viet Nam compliance with government regulations is often simply considered the right thing to do.

Avoiding fines and harassment was the most immediate benefit of compliance mentioned by many MSEs in the surveys – in the United Republic of Tanzania, for example, this was the most-mentioned reason for registration with the tax authorities. Relatively few enterprises perceive any other benefits arising from compliance. This coincides with some previous studies that show that the benefits of formality may not be visible to MSEs (Maldonado et al., 1999).

As we have seen earlier in this chapter, compliance rates vary between micro- and small enterprises. Encouraging micro- or survivalist enterprises to comply with business regulations can involve a different set of issues to those concerning small enterprises. Micro-enterprises can be encouraged toward official compliance by easing entry into the enterprise sector through the simplification of official processes, the lowering of costs, and so forth. On the other hand, small enterprises may be more interested in the strategic benefits of compliance, such as access to resources, ability to sign contracts, and possible export opportunities.

Some of the potential benefits of formality only become relevant in the medium and long term, and may not even be immediately visible or desirable. Compliance with tax regulations, for example, is clearly a cost in the short run but may have the positive side effect of improving the accounting system and thus the business strategy of the enterprise (Tokman et al., 2001). Obtaining a permit to operate within a given location provides a degree of security to the enterprise, and in turn may facilitate access to credit. Compliance also helps with access to the legal and judicial system to enforce contracts, and gives better access to public infrastructure (such as utilities and secure premises) and benefits.

In their competition for resources, informal enterprises are at a disadvantaged position compared to formal enterprises. Compliance facilitates access to inputs, improves an enterprise's legitimacy in the industry, creates a reputation of trustworthiness in the eyes of clients and suppliers, and makes the enterprise less vulnerable to corruption and harassment (Goedhuys, 2002). All these benefits tend to give enterprises that comply with regulations better market access than enterprises that do not comply (see box 3.4). Once a business is registered, the trading name is protected and the enterprise can begin to advertise and build a commercial demand for their brand of service or product. Indeed, the most frequently mentioned problem associated with non-compliance in a survey of Peruvian MSEs was restricted market access (Robles et al., 2001).

The policy environment has a key role in ensuring that MSEs are not excluded from the potential benefits of compliance. Registration, for example, might mean that an MSE owner-manager can apply to a commercial bank for a loan, but no credit will be extended without collateral. Copyright certificates might allow an enterprise the right to sell genuine articles under a patent, but if others can produce and sell the cheaper fake, then this right is meaningless. Thus, the enabling functions of laws and regulations need to offer tangible and realistic benefits to MSE owner-managers.

In the perception of MSE owners and managers, the costs of compliance in many cases outweigh the benefits. This may be because regulations are poorly designed and implemented, making compliance unnecessarily expensive while restricting its benefits. Another important factor for many MSEs is the lack of information. Information on short-term costs may be more readily available than information on potential medium- and long-term benefits. Obtaining information on how to comply with the regulations may often involve a substantial cost for an MSE, in addition to the cost of complying itself. Moreover, most MSEs have to rely on informal sources of information, while more formal sources of information are often beyond their reach.

The role of information

According to the MSE surveys, the two major sources of business advice were the same in most countries: newspapers, friends and family. There were no significant differences

Box 3.4   The benefits of compliance: Cases from the Philippines

In order to illustrate the costs and benefits of formalization, the ILO commissioned a series of case studies on enterprises in the Philippines that first operated informally and then formalized. Another series of case studies was conducted on enterprises that used to be formal and went informal.

One garment enterprise in particular illustrates the benefits of formalization. During 1992 and 1993, the owner, a female university graduate, made several attempts to start her business informally but each time ran into severe difficulties. One of the problems was that dealers and boutique owners would fail to pay their accounts. She had to run after them to collect her receivables, but many did not pay.

By 1995, she wanted to legalize her business, even though she strongly disliked transacting with government offices. Big clients were asking for invoices, receipts and other legal documents to support her contracts with them. She also needed an income tax return in order to have a credit line. She mobilized her accountant to deal with the tax and social security authorities, and used another acquaintance to facilitate the payment of her quarterly business fees and obtaining the yearly permit with the local authorities. Despite the trouble and inconvenience, she did not regret formalizing her business, which was now able to access bigger markets and grow rapidly.

While this and other cases illustrate the benefit of compliance through better market access and better protection against dishonest practices of business partners, other enterprises that had formalized at some stage went informal to cut costs on taxes and fees. In all cases, however, informalization was a mere survival strategy that did not result in a successful business.

Source: ILO, unpublished case studies on the informal sector in the Philippines, 1995.

between micro- and small enterprises or between men and women in this regard. The possibility of obtaining advice from legal specialists is heavily dependent on the size of the enterprise. While in the countries under study, only 1 to 10 per cent of micro-enterprises in the MSE surveys mentioned "lawyer or legal specialist" as a source of information, this share was substantially higher among the small enterprises, reaching as much as 35 per cent in Peru.

Thus, the costs of information are an important element in MSEs' decisions to comply with government regulations. The lack of information may also be an explanation for the apparent contradiction that MSEs perceive more costs than benefits from compliance, while, as described below, more formal MSEs often turn out to grow more than their less formal counterparts.

The literature on the link between regulations and employment often emphasizes the possibly negative impact of regulations on the employment potential of MSEs. However, despite the complaints of many MSE owner-managers about cumbersome or inadequate laws and regulations, enterprises that were more formal were found to create more employment than their more informal counterparts, all other things being equal. There was an advantage to being formal, in being recognized by government and other market actors, which helped these enterprises gather the resources required to create more employment than their informal peers.

Compliance with regulations can help enterprises to develop and create more employment

Imagine two small enterprises of similar size, economic sector and entrepreneur characteristics. One of them complies with most government regulations, while the other does not. Considering only the cost of compliance, we would expect the more informal enterprise to grow faster than the more formal one. Yet, statistically, in most countries it is the more formal enterprise that grows faster and has a stronger growth of employment. Among the seven countries studied, a significant positive relationship between registration and employment growth was found in Chile, Peru and South Africa. Statistically, registration raised the probability that an MSE has grown from 70 per cent to 85 per cent in Peru, from 12 per cent to 28 per cent in Chile and from 33 per cent to 59 per cent in South Africa. This positive correlation was strongly significant for the overall sample (Christensen and Goedhuys, forthcoming).[2]

Other studies have also found that more formal enterprises grow faster in Burundi, Côte d'Ivoire, Mexico, Peru and the United Republic of Tanzania, while Cameroon displayed the

---

[2] See table A.9 in the Annex. In Guinea, the United Republic of Tanzania and Viet Nam, the correlation coefficient was slightly negative, but not statistically significant. Pakistan could not be included due to lacking data. Some methodological caveats apply. First, the MSE surveys include information on compliance in only the final year for which data were collected (2001), rather than the beginning period (1999). Second, enterprises that register may also be better organized in other aspects, creating a selection bias. Therefore, the causality from better compliance to more employment creation may be the other way around in some cases: because an enterprise grew and created more employment, it was likely to register. Despite these caveats, the results from this and other studies suggest that, at the very least, compliance with regulations is not an obstacle to employment creation.

opposite relationship, with informal enterprises growing more than formal (Levenson and Maloney, 1998; Goedhuys and Sleuwaegen, 1999; Robles et al., 2001; Goedhuys, 2002). These results illustrate that the benefits of compliance – access to markets, resources and incentive schemes – on average outweigh the costs of compliance.

There appear to be two main reasons why compliance can contribute to employment growth. Firstly, it is an indication of commitment. Many people in developing countries establish their own business because there are no other options open to them. Such people may have been unsuccessful in finding employment in the public sector or within larger employers. They may also have been unemployed for some time and because of financial strains establish their own enterprise. In some cases this is a stopgap measure, and as soon as an alternative opportunity arises, they will leave the enterprise. Such people are less likely to go through the processes required to formalize their enterprise. Many are unable to obtain the financial resources to comply, while others may be completely unaware of the demands of the State in this regard. It is likely that those enterprise owner-managers who do make the effort to comply with state requirements and are successful in doing so have indicated a stronger long-term commitment to their enterprise.

The second reason that compliance contributes to employment growth concerns the access to resources. Compliance with the State provides formality and recognition to small enterprises. This offers a number of practical and substantial benefits to small enterprises, which can aid them in their growth. For example, properly registered enterprises may be eligible for state incentive schemes. They are also more likely to obtain access to finance from formal financial institutions such as banks. While physical collateral and experience in business remain common constraints to bank finance, the legal recognition of an enterprise can make the bank more comfortable. Insurance is a similar example. In most countries, MSEs are unable to insure their business and their workers unless they are formally recognized by state authorities, usually by complying with some kind of registration process.

The positive potential for compliance in contributing to MSE employment illustrates the power of compliance as a tool for development. An effective policy and legal framework should facilitate the movement of MSEs out of the margins and into the mainstream of the economy. Laws and regulations, while enshrining socially sanctioned obligations and restrictions on enterprise behaviour, can also facilitate the development of MSEs by providing them with rights and improving their access to the broader economy.

3.3 Compliance as a means for development

Compliance with the policy and legal environment is often seen as a desirable achievement by governments, who set the rules and employ significant resources to implement them. It is often assumed that compliance is a reflection of the well-being and status of an enterprise. However, our findings lead us to the view that compliance can be used as a tool for development rather than a measuring stick. When they are properly designed and administered, government policies, laws and regulations can be used to enhance the development potential of the MSE sector, rather than as a means to simply filter out less desirable enterprises.

Governments and MSE stakeholders can encourage compliance with regulations as a means of development

Regardless of their size, successful enterprises often succeed despite the laws and regulations of the day because capable, enterprising people run them. However, our concern is with those MSEs that are in, or close to, the margins of success (or viability), as well as with laws and regulations that unnecessarily draw resources from the enterprise. MSEs need to generate profits and maintain the levels of productivity required to remain competitive within increasingly competitive markets. Legal and regulatory frameworks can facilitate this process by creating an environment in which MSEs can respond to market changes and enhance their competitiveness.

When it comes to the content of policies and laws themselves, governments can become more responsive to the circumstances and capacities of MSEs while appreciating the need for appropriate standards and conditions that protect all enterprises, their workers, their customers and society at large. There are a number of issues that governments must balance. Most of these concern the design of policies and laws that recognize the limited resources of small enterprises, while ensuring that they act in a responsible manner within these constraints.

MSEs can be encouraged to formalize by reducing the cost of compliance

It is not possible to investigate thoroughly the impact of specific policies and laws on employment in MSEs in this study. However, we are able to identify two kinds of approaches that governments can use in tandem to influence the decisions of MSE owner-managers and enable them to reap the potential benefits of compliance: reducing the burdens of compliance, and increasing its advantages.

Reducing the costs of the regulatory system has the effect of increasing compliance rates by MSEs. This brings with it employment benefits, and can be done without reducing labour standards. Reducing regulatory costs is an important development tool, because these costs are a commonly cited reason why owner-managers avoid their legal obligations. Specifically, governments can try to reduce the costs incurred in the administration of state policies and laws. These costs are not associated with the actual standards that the State desires, such as the costs an enterprise incurs to insure its workers, make its workplace safe or maintain an appropriate level of hygiene.

Some of the ways governments can reduce the costs of administering government policies and laws include:

- reducing fees and other costs, including both initial registration costs and ongoing payments required to remain formal;
- streamlining regulatory procedures, sometimes by centralizing or improving the coordination of multiple government agencies (for example, creating centralized "one-stop shops");
- setting up government agencies for registration and information close to where MSEs are situated, so as to spare them expensive and time-consuming travel;
- using the Internet where appropriate to carry out administrative interactions online;
- introducing self-reporting schemes where appropriate to reduce the number of inspection visits;
- contracting business associations for procedures and service delivery where this is more cost-effective.

The second approach to influence the decisions of MSE owner-managers in favour of compliance concerns the benefits that formalization can offer. Governments have to respond to the demands of the MSE sector with benefits that are both meaningful and pragmatic. This approach should complement efforts to make the legal and regulatory environment more MSE friendly, by making it more conducive to the efficient operations of the enterprise.

> A conducive policy and legal environment lowers the costs to establish and operate a business, including simplified registration and licensing procedures, appropriate rules and regulations, reasonable and fair taxation. It also increases the benefits of legal registration, facilitating access to commercial buyers, more favourable credit terms, legal protection, contract enforcement, access to technology, subsidies, foreign exchange and local and international markets. Besides, such policies discourage businesses in the formal economy from shifting into the informal economy. This helps new businesses to start and smaller businesses to enter the formal economy and to create new jobs, without lowering labour standards. This also increases state revenues. (ILO, 2002a)

To increase the benefits of compliance with regulations, governments and other stakeholders should ensure that MSEs have access to infrastructure and benefit schemes, notably in the area of trade policies, investment policies and innovation policies. Wherever appropriate, minimum thresholds of turnover, exports or investments should be avoided so that smaller enterprises can apply for benefits under the same conditions as larger enterprises. Whenever possible, the legal status attained through compliance with regulations should qualify enterprises for access to benefits. Moreover, the delivery of services and infrastructure, which is often biased in favour of larger enterprises, should be reviewed so as to improve MSE access.

Giving MSEs full access to infrastructure and incentive schemes increases the benefits of compliance

Compliance with regulations is generally reflected in better job quality for MSE workers through social protection and certain minimum standards. This in itself has a potential for increased labour productivity through lower labour turnover and stronger commitment of workers to their enterprise. In addition, training policies should help MSEs to train their workers and increase their skill level. This can help enterprises to enhance their productivity and competitiveness. More specific biases against small enterprises and examples of good practice to ensure a level playing field for enterprises of all size classes are discussed in the corresponding subsections of Chapter 4.

The role of local The two-pronged approach to MSE compliance has an
government added spatial dimension, represented by the different levels
of government. While much of the discussion in this chapter
has focused on the role of national laws and regulations, the
role of subnational authorities is particularly significant to
MSE operations. In all the countries we investigated, district,
provincial or local levels of government were found to have
great influence on MSEs. Thus, the creation of an effective
legal and regulatory framework for MSE employment
requires a high degree of coordination and harmonization
across these levels of government. Concurrent to this,
subnational government authorities should be assisted in
designing laws and regulations that are conducive to the
growth of more and better jobs in their local MSE sector.
One of the most interesting examples of local authorities that
have taken a fresh approach to dealing with the compliance
requirements on MSEs and the informal economy in
particular can be found in the city of Durban in South
Africa (box 3.5).

Box 3.5   Informal economy policy in Durban, South Africa

Policy on the informal economy in Durban illustrates how local stakeholders can formulate
proposals to improve the environment for micro-enterprises and other operators in the
informal economy. The main innovations in dealing with the informal economy in South
Africa lie in the representation of the informal economy in the policy arena, as well as in
the shift from a repressive to an enabling role of government.

As the city of Durban was developing its vision of a new urban policy and institutional
framework, it found that one of the problems was that there were too many different
departments and agencies dealing with different aspects of urban governance. It also
found that the MSE sector, which is largely informal, made a significant contribution to the
economic and social life of the city. As a result, Durban decided in 2000 to develop a
comprehensive written policy for the informal economy, which is "pro-development" in
that it dovetails with the economic development of the city. In preparing this policy, the
city consulted broadly with key groups in a highly participatory manner. The resulting
policy is targeted at the poorest segments of the informal economy, such as street
vendors and home workers, and combines area-based management with sector-based
support to MSEs. For street vendors, concrete steps agreed upon include identification

cards to provide legitimization for their work; clearly marked and numbered places for them to market their goods and services; and provision of night-time storage facilities near their places of work.

When dealing with informal economy issues the city seeks to promote synergies between the formal and informal economies, including dealing with both formal and informal economy issues in the same institutional structures and processes. The policy also emphasizes the organization of informal actors because it recognizes that the interests of the informal actors are best served when they can bargain from a position of strength and confidence and that the interests of local government are best served when there are strong and stable partners to negotiate with.

Source: Durban City Council (2000).

Spreading information makes MSEs more aware of the benefits of compliance Improving the legal and regulatory environment in which MSEs operate – by reducing the costs and increasing the benefits of compliance – will not create the desired positive impact if MSE owner-managers do not know about these changes. It is therefore essential to inform MSEs about reforms and the necessary steps for compliance. This should involve the distribution of clear and easy-to-understand information on regulatory requirements and steps of compliance, as well as the use of mass media campaigns to raise awareness (through television, radio and the Internet, for example). Better communication and cooperation between government and MSE associations, as well as employer organizations and member-based NGOs, can also enhance the outreach of information. Again, mass media has an important role to play in this regard (see box 3.6).

This chapter has discussed how policies and regulations can contribute to MSE growth and employment creation. In the following chapter, we will analyse six policy areas in more detail to identify common problems and examples of good practice.

Box 3.6   Giving businesspeople a voice in policy development and implementation:
            Radio programmes in Africa

Mass media can be a powerful platform for policy debate and formulation. Until recently, the media in sub-Saharan Africa was predominantly government controlled, but over the last decade deregulation has brought an explosion of small private radio stations across the continent. These radio stations have offered for the first time not only a source of information, but also a platform for public debate and a channel for a two-way flow of information and exchange of opinions.

ILO/SEED has tapped into the potential of the radio media to inform and represent the informal economy and the MSE sector. ILO/SEED has supported commercial radio stations in Ghana and Uganda to devise, launch and run profitable, and therefore sustainable, weekly radio programmes that target the huge informal and small business sectors. The programme formats are demand-led and the producers have quickly realized that there is a huge demand for radio programmes that highlight and tackle policy issues that affect the day-to-day operation of MSEs. The resulting small business current affairs programmes are a mix of investigative reporting, interviews, live debate and phone-ins.

The first of the programmes to be launched was Nekolera Gyange, in Central Uganda. In early 2000, the Ugandan Government announced that it was banning the small-scale vending of milk. Nekolera Gyange investigated the issue on behalf of the thousands of milk traders, transporters and dairy farmers who would lose their livelihoods. According to Member of Parliament Hon. Kityo Mutebi, the radio programme was instrumental in reversing the ban. Rather than banning small-scale milk vending, the Government embarked on a plan to regulate and improve safety standards, thus saving thousands of jobs.

The same radio programme also helped the Government to implement policy. For example, a ban on fish exports to the European Union from Lake Victoria came about because of a combination of poor fish livestock and environmental management and poor fishing and processing practices, and resulted in considerable hardship for the hundreds of fishing communities spread along the Lake's shores. The Ugandan Government embarked on a policy of tightening up and enforcing fishing regulations as a step towards lifting the ban, but this move was construed among the fishermen as an additional hardship enforced by government officials on the already suffering fishing communities. The issue was taken up by the radio, giving both the fishermen and the Government a platform to present and discuss the problems and proposed solutions. The programme had a significant effect in breaking down the divisions between the two sides. "Thanks to Nekolera Gyange," stated one fisheries official, "When I go to explain to the fishermen how to clean and process their fish, they now listen."

Through the public dialogue created by the radio programme the Government began to be perceived as an ally in reversing the ban and fishing communities began to collaborate with enforcing fishing regulations. As one fisherman commented soon after the ban had been lifted: "We have to keep our eyes open the whole night to guard against any malpractice on the lake – especially people using wrong size nets and poison to fish... If what happened to us during the ban reoccurs I will not be able to pay school fees for my children."

As these two examples show, radio programmes can provide MSEs with a unique channel through which they can both influence and understand policy issues. In countries with liberalized media, they can become an integral part of policy development processes and improve policy design and implementation.

Source: Gavin Anderson, ILO/SEED and FIT Africa, based on impact analysis of radio programmes for MSEs in Uganda and Ghana.

ASSESSING THE POLICY AND LEGAL ENVIRONMENT

4

The policy and legal environment affecting employment in MSEs is the sum of intended and unintended influences stemming from the design and the implementation of policies and laws, and from the procedures, mechanisms and institutions required to execute them. This environment results from specific micro- and macro-policies, but is also shaped by the far broader fields of governance and the structure of the State.

Six policy fields affecting employment in MSEs are assessed in this chapter. This assessment deals with both the design and implementation dimensions of policy, adopting a two-step process. We review first the policy fields, and then investigate the combined impact of these policy fields on the broader business environment.

4.1 Review of key policy fields

The six fields of policy investigated in this study have been chosen because of their relevance to MSE activities. They are:

- specific small enterprise promotion policies;
- business laws and regulations;
- taxation policies, laws and regulations;
- labour policies, laws and regulations;
- trade policies;
- finance and credit policies, laws and regulations.

Legal and political systems vary across countries. In general terms, however, three levels of government activity can be distinguished: policies and laws, regulations, and administrative mechanisms (box 4.1).

Box 4.1   From policies to administrative mechanisms: Layers of the policy
environment for MSEs

Regardless of the system of government, there are three general layers of government
activity that shape the environment for MSEs. These are, first, the policies and laws that
set the directions and intentions of government. Policies and laws are the exercise of a
sovereign power. They underpin development efforts and influence the role MSEs are able
to perform while providing the basis for regulatory action. Policies, like all the other fields
of government activity, can be developed at national, regional and local levels. In countries
where the system of government is based on a British tradition, policy documents may
be called a "White Paper" (as in South Africa) or simply a "policy" (as in the United
Republic of Tanzania). In other countries, a Presidential Decree (as in Viet Nam) or a law
(as in Peru) may set the policy orientation on small enterprise development. Legislation
may be passed by a parliament or congress – sometimes there are two houses of
parliament through which a bill must pass. In some systems, bills require presidential or
royal assert before they become law. Laws may take the shape of published statutes, or
cabinet, congressional or presidential decrees.

Following on from this, there are regulations. These are the means through which policies
and laws are implemented. Regulations are the principal acts, rules or procedural
directives issued by administrative agencies to implement laws. These agencies must
have specific authorization to issue directives and must usually adhere to procedures and
conditions that are prescribed by the parliament or congress. Regulations represent the
"tools" that are used to enact the policies and legislation in the pursuit of desired
outcomes.

Finally, there are administrative mechanisms through which policies and laws, and their
implementing regulations, are delivered. Administration governs the operations of
institutions and refers to the ways in which policies, laws and regulations are applied,
managed, enforced and monitored. There are many policies and laws at the national level
that affect MSEs, and increasingly local governments are required to administer these.

Three broad criteria were used to assess each of the
selected policy fields. The first criterion considers the extent to
which policies, laws and regulations recognize enterprises of
different size classes. The second criterion examines the
manner in which policies, laws and regulations are implemented, and the role that institutions play in this regard.
Finally, the third area of assessment focuses on the impact that
these policies, laws and regulations have on MSE establishment, operations and employment decisions.

The first major assessment criterion is the degree to which policies accommodate the requirements of MSEs. While some policies may be specifically designed for enterprises of particular size classes, others will refer generally to private enterprises. Generic policies may initially appear to be size-neutral, but their application and impact will often be biased in favour of or against certain categories of enterprises. Where a policy does specify enterprises of a particular kind, the definitions that are applied and the criteria used to identify micro-, small and medium-sized enterprises are of interest. Depending on the country, policy texts may refer to "micro- and small enterprises", "household enterprises", "small and medium-sized enterprises", "the handicraft sector", or "artisans".

Assessing the responsiveness of policies and laws to MSEs

Using this criterion to assess policies required answers to questions such as:

- Do policies, laws and regulations provide for a differential treatment of enterprises by size class?
- Are MSE policies based on a clear understanding of the current and potential role of MSEs in the economy?
- Do current policies and laws appear to reflect current conditions, or are they out-dated remnants from the past?
- Did the MSE sector participate in the process of policy design? Were their representative agencies engaged in dialogue with government on these matters?
- Are there any signs that these policies and laws affect women and men differently? Is there any difference in the way women-owned enterprises and men-owned enterprises are treated?

A particular interest within this criterion is the extent of segmentation or targeting. It may be, for example, that export-oriented enterprises are targeted for support and promotion, or enterprises that involve a high proportion of poor people are promoted in an effort to use enterprise promotion as part of a broader poverty reduction strategy. It is also common to find policies that focus on the manufacturing sector, while policies dealing with trade and service enterprises are far less common.

Using this criterion to assess policies required answers to questions such as:

- Which sub-sectors of the MSE sector have been given more policy attention by government and why?

- Are there any special policies that support the development of women-owned enterprises or enterprises owned by young people or people from indigenous groups?

Assessing institutions and procedures for implementation

The second major assessment criterion applied in this investigation addressed the institutions for turning policy directives into reality and the procedural and administrative arrangements that are established by these institutions. Assessing policies based on the institutions used for implementation required answers to questions such as:

- What kinds of specific attention has government given to the creation of institutions that respond to MSE needs (for example, a ministry of small business, government recognition of MSE representative and advocacy organizations, one-stop shops for MSEs)?
- Have the institutions for policy implementation been sufficiently empowered – financially, technically and politically?
- Can the institutions for policy implementation be adequately accessed by both women and men, and by enterprise owner-managers that are located in rural areas as well as in urban areas?
- Are the institutions for policy implementation responsive to the calls of the MSE sector?
- Has government created any institutions for policy implementation (and design and review) that involve representatives of the MSE sector?

While the design and adoption of policy instruments might reflect the intentions of government, the process of implementation may distort this image and blur the intentions of government. Procedural and administrative arrangements are often created by officials within government institutions who may not adopt the views or directions of those who originally designed the policy or law. These arrangements have a direct influence on the impact of a policy on the MSE sector and can change its outcomes dramatically.

Assessing procedural and administrative arrangements includes addressing questions such as:

- Are any of the procedural and administrative arrangements directly or indirectly biased against MSEs and in favour of medium-sized or large enterprises?

- Are administrative decisions made on the basis of objective criteria, or are they arbitrary or lacking transparency?
- Is corruption widespread?
- How do MSEs find out about their compliance obligations, responsibilities and rights within these policy fields?
- Have special efforts been made in this regard (for example, information campaigns, centralized information in one single government office)?
- What monitoring and review mechanisms have been established to determine if the policy is working and how it can be improved?

Finally, this assessment of policy fields sought to identify any of the ways that these policies created an impact on MSEs.

Assessing the impact on MSEs

- Did more or fewer MSEs start up as a result of a particular policy intervention?
- Did MSEs do better – did they grow – as a result of a particular policy intervention?
- Did MSE employment increase and did the quality of MSE employment improve?

Assessing the impact of a specific policy intervention on the MSE sector is difficult because this intervention alone is hard to distinguish from others. Not only can other policy interventions influence this impact – either by enhancing or dampening the effect of the single policy under assessment – so too can the broader business environment and changes in the market-place. Thus, some of the following questions were used to assess the possible impact of a single policy:

- What is the expected impact of specific policy interventions?
- Have there been other studies conducted that assess the impact of a specific policy intervention on the MSE sector? Has the government, private sector, or trade union movement made any claims in this regard?
- Are there any indications that the impact of policies and laws varies for women or men, or between women-owned enterprises and men-owned enterprises?
- Is there any evidence of compliance by MSEs with laws and regulations (for example, the share of registered versus unregistered MSEs)? Does this appear to vary according to industrial sub-sectors, the actors involved or specific target groups?

4.1.1 Specific small enterprise promotion policies

Many countries have taken the initiative to formulate national policies, varied in scope, that address the concerns of private enterprises directly. The interest for our research was the extent to which governments formulated enterprise promotion policies that focused on the small enterprise sector, including the self-employed and micro-enterprises. In cases where such policies exist, we were interested in their coverage at the lower end of the size class spectrum.

Specific small enterprise policies exist in a number of countries

Small and medium-sized enterprise (SME) promotion policies represent the official government approach to the promotion of MSEs. Such policies are emerging in a number of countries. Among the countries under study, Chile, Peru, South Africa and Viet Nam already have some kind of specific small enterprise policy; efforts to formulate such a policy are under way in Guinea and in the United Republic of Tanzania (box 4.2). This illustrates a growing interest in the sector and its contribution to national development goals.

Specific small enterprise policies provide the opportunity to cover a range of topics related to small enterprise development in one document. This includes the provision of financial and business development services, incentive schemes to foster enterprise creation and growth, and a regulatory environment that is "small enterprise friendly". As such, the policy document can be comprehensive and provide a framework for reforms in a number of policy fields affecting MSEs.

Official definitions of MSEs vary by country

Small enterprise promotion policies are often a useful instrument for defining the MSE sector (box 4.3). Usually this is done by criteria that include the number of employees, annual turnover, registered capital, and power usage. While in most countries the small enterprise sector is – by definition or de facto – limited to private enterprises, in Viet Nam it includes small or medium-sized state-owned enterprises. Some countries do not have official MSE definitions, but use definitions at a lower administrative level for specific purposes, such as the compilation of statistical data. For example, in Pakistan, the Census of Establishments in 1988 defined micro-enterprises as public and private enterprises with one to nine employees, small enterprises ten to 49

Box 4.2   Overview of specific small enterprise policies

Chile   The policy statement "The President's 12 Commitments to the SME Sector" (2000) could lead to the formulation of a more elaborate SME policy. A public–private sector committee on the SME sector has been meeting. Several other of the 12 commitments have already been implemented.

Guinea   No specific small enterprise policy yet. A multidisciplinary and multi-sectoral Technical Committee for Policy Formulation was established in 2000 and is considering the need for an MSE policy.

Pakistan   No specific small enterprise policy yet.

Peru   Law No. 27268: General Law on Small and Micro Enterprises (2000) and Regulation of the General Law on Small and Micro Enterprises (2000). The Law and its Regulation cover a wide range of MSE matters, including regulations, training, business development services, innovations and finance marketing. However, there are still some concerns regarding implementation.

South Africa   White Paper on National Strategy for the Development and Promotion of Small Business in South Africa (1995) and National Small Business Act (1996). The National Small Business Act defines small, micro- and medium enterprises (SMMEs) and establishes a set of institutions. Government departments are encouraged (but not compelled) to assess the impact of policies and laws on MSEs.

Tanzania   No specific small enterprise policy yet, although a draft policy entitled SME Development Policy of the United Republic of Tanzania has been circulating for some time and is due to be passed soon.

Viet Nam   The Decree on Supporting the Development of Small and Medium Enterprises (2001) creates new support schemes for SMEs, such as the creation of a Technical Assistance Centre, and a government department to provide support to SMEs, as well as a new SME Council that includes private-sector representatives.

Sources: Country papers and ILO/SEED: *Documentation of small enterprise policies, laws and regulations*, http://www.ilo.org/seed.

employees, medium-sized enterprises 50 to 99 employees, and large enterprises with 100 or more employees. The definitions used in the seven countries are summarized in box 4.3.

Box 4.3	Overview of enterprise size definitions
Chile	No official definition exists. Administrative definitions are used for tax purposes (based on turnover) and for other statistical purposes (based on employment size).
Guinea	The Framework Programme Supporting the Development of the Private Sector (1998) gives the following definition:
	Micro-enterprise: 1 to 3 employees; assets below 10 million Guinean francs and turnover below 15 million; management by the owner and rudimentary organization.
	Small and medium-sized enterprise: Up to 60 employees; assets up to 300 million Guinean francs and turnover up to 500 million; management by the owner or delegated; modest organizational structure.
	Large enterprise: More than 60 employees; assets over 300 Guinean francs and turnover over 500 million; well-structured organization.
	The Investment Code (1998) gives a different definition based on assets, number of permanent employees and the existence of a formal accounting system.
Pakistan	No official definition exists. Administrative definitions based on employment are used for statistical purposes.
Peru	The General Law on Small and Micro Enterprises (2000) gives the following definitions:
	Micro-enterprise: 1 to 10 workers.
	Small enterprise: 11 to 40 workers.
South Africa	According to the National Small Business Act (1996), the definition of enterprises in terms of employment, total annual turnover and total gross asset value varies for different sectors and subsectors. The Act gives the following generic definition:
	Micro-enterprise: 0 to 5 employees and informal accounting and operating procedures.
	Very small enterprise: 6 to 10 employees.
	Small enterprise: 11 to 50 employees.
	Medium-sized enterprise: 51 to 99 employees.

Tanzania	No official definition exists. The current draft of the SME Policy proposes the following definitions:
	Micro-enterprises: 1 to 4 employees; 0 to 5 million Tanzanian shillings of investment, and 0 to 12 million shillings turnover.
	Small enterprises: 5 to 49 employees, over 5 million and up to 200 million Tanzanian shillings of investment, and a turnover of up to 150 million.
	Medium-sized enterprises: 50 to 100 employees, over 200 million and up to 800 million Tanzanian shillings of investment, and a turnover of up to 300 million.
	Large enterprises: More than 100 employees; more than 800 million Tanzanian shillings of investment, and a turnover of more than 300 million.
Viet Nam	The Decree on Supporting the Development of Small and Medium Enterprises (2001) defines small and medium enterprises as independent business and production establishments that have registered their business under the current legislation and have a registered capital of less than 10 billion Vietnamese dollars or an average of fewer than 300 annual employees.

Source: Country papers. For an alternative presentation with further details, see table A.1 in the Annex.

Small enterprise policies do not always address the specific problems of men and women and of micro-enterprises

Many enterprise promotion policies focus on small and medium-sized enterprises while overlooking the concerns of self-employed and micro-enterprises – those at the lower end of the enterprise size spectrum. Micro-enterprises are often seen as being less significant and less deserving of government attention. In some cases, the micro-enterprise sector is synonymous with the informal economy. In South Africa, for example, micro-enterprises are often placed in the category of "survivalist" enterprise. Thus, micro-enterprises often fall under social policies.

Another weakness in the design of many MSE promotion policies is that, despite the high levels of participation of women in MSEs in most countries, the different needs of female and male enterprise owner-managers are rarely recognized. The recent decree on small and medium enterprises in Viet Nam (see box 4.2), for example, does not refer to gender dimensions of small enterprise development.

Many small enterprise policies fail to be implemented and coordinated with other existing policies

In many countries, the lack of a clear implementation strategy that considers institutions and mechanisms has contributed to the limited impact of MSE policies. Implementation often suffers from a lack of work schedules and time frames, as well as from an unclear distribution of responsibilities. Moreover, the coordination between specific small enterprise promotion policies and other existing policies is often poor. The United Republic of Tanzania currently faces this challenge. Very ambitious policy documents are already in place, dealing with industrial development, employment and gender equity, and a draft SME policy is also being finalized. The Government, in cooperation with relevant stakeholders, must now harmonize these different policy documents and find adequate mechanisms for implementation.

An essential aspect of implementation is information dissemination. Most MSEs never obtain the information on the available programmes that are provided for their benefit. In a survey among small enterprises in Bangladesh, Nepal and the Philippines, more than 70 per cent of the surveyed entrepreneurs did not know about any public agency in their country giving assistance to small enterprises (Meier and Pilgrim, 1994, p. 37). Likewise, the recent SME policy statement in Chile (see box 4.2) was only known to one-fifth of the enterprises in our survey sample (Espinosa, 2001).

These problems of poor implementation are not unique to MSE policies, or to any of the policy fields described in this chapter. Many developing countries experience difficulties when rising to the challenge of effective implementation and, as a result, well-intentioned and even well-designed policies are rarely realized.

The processes of implementation are reliant on strong and efficient institutions. Government institutions of all kinds are required to improve their capacity for governance, but also to recognize the range of influences that shape the broader business environment. Successful MSE promotion requires, among other things, markets that MSEs can access, an institutional framework for financial and business development services, political commitment by government, and a mechanism for effective representation and advocacy by the MSE sector. Thus, implementation of a single policy occurs among a range of competing and divergent influences.

Most small enterprise policies are primarily concerned with the promotion of small enterprises. This usually involves three areas of intervention: the creation of an enabling environment, the use of financial and non-financial instruments for business development, and the establishment of institutions to represent, promote and support small enterprises. All of the small enterprise promotion policies reviewed in this study address these issues to varying degrees. The policy framework for small enterprise promotion in South Africa, for example, highlights the role of institutions in the representation of small enterprises, as well as a mechanism for the delivery of financial and non-financial services to MSEs (see box 4.4). Similarly, in Viet Nam special consideration has been given to the establishment of a new department for SMEs.

There have been a number of financial and business development services found within the countries we studied. Some of these have been mandated by a small enterprise promotion policy, but most have been developed through programme efforts of line ministries or enterprise promotion agencies, including public, private and community-based agencies. Over the last decade, a great deal of work has been undertaken to assess and improve the work of agencies engaged in the delivery of financial and business development services for MSEs. Significantly, this has led to further debates regarding the role of government in small enterprise promotion.[1]

Financial services and business development services

Effective small enterprise development makes use of markets, and government should intervene where necessary to address market inequities and distortions. On this basis, the role of governments in facilitating financial and business development services is broadly acknowledged. However, it is generally recognized that the principal role of government is "to provide an enabling policy, legal and regulatory environment for small enterprises and business development service providers, as well as public goods such as basic infrastructure, education and information services"; governments can also play a vital role in promoting "more vibrant service markets" (Tanburn et al., 2001).

---

[1] See, for example, publications of the Committee of Donor Agencies for Small Enterprise Development (1995; 1997; 2001) and Tanburn et al. (2001).

The challenge for institutions to match high expectations

Getting the institutions right remains a serious challenge, as box 4.4 illustrates with the example of South Africa. It has proved extremely difficult to fulfil the enormous expectations for specific small enterprise promotion policies if they do not lead to broader policy reform in various fields of economic policy, including strategies for implementation at the local level. Indeed, the fact that specific MSE policies can be a useful framework for reform implies that they cannot provide solutions by themselves. Rather, they can serve as a tool to start a process of improving the policy and legal environment and establishing mechanisms to provide services to these enterprises.

Small enterprise policies cannot by themselves create a more conducive policy environment

Small enterprise policies can be used to establish a mechanism whereby new economic laws and regulations are screened for their potential impact on the MSE sector before they are enacted. The Regulatory Flexibility Act (1980) and the Small Business Regulatory Enforcement Fairness Act (1996) in the United States, for example, require agencies to collect inputs from small enterprises to determine whether new regulations are expected to have a significant economic impact on this category of enterprises. Moreover, government agencies are required to publish compliance guides that explain in plain language how small enterprises should comply with regulations.

In the countries under study, only a few policies include similar provisions. In South Africa, the National Small Business Act (1996) encourages government departments to assess the impact of policies and laws on MSEs and a detailed impact assessment study was carried out before deciding on the application of the Basic Conditions of Employment Act (1997) to MSEs. Although not compulsory in South Africa, this is an example of good practice (see box 4.8 on page 99). In general, most specific small enterprise policies do not give enough attention to measures that can create a more conducive legal and regulatory environment for business development and the creation and improvement of employment.

Because of the influence of the broader range of policies and laws, along with the influence of the business environment, it has been difficult to establish their impact beyond specific interventions (such as the incentives for innovations in Chile mentioned above). No evidence was found directly

Box 4.4   Institutions for small enterprise policies in South Africa

A range of institutions in South Africa focus on the promotion of small enterprises – referred to as small, micro- and medium enterprises (SMMEs). The White Paper on National Strategy for the Development and Promotion of Small Business in South Africa (1995), which was followed by the National Small Business Act (1996), created a formal structure to address the concerns and needs of the small enterprise sector through the creation of three institutions that were supervised by the Department of Trade and Industry. The first of these was the National Small Business Council – a membership organization which was to represent and promote the interests of small business and advise the national, provincial and local spheres of government on social and economic policy that promotes the development of small business. The second institution formed was Khula Enterprise Finance Ltd. – a micro-financing institution for SMMEs. The third institution was the Ntsika Enterprise Promotion Agency, a national agency established to provide non-financial support through a national network of local business support centres.

Despite these important efforts, the institutional framework brought about by the 1996 Act has struggled with the challenges of implementation. The National Small Business Council was meant to have taken on a strong advocacy role on behalf of SMMEs from all sectors, but is now defunct. Its generic role in proactively acting to support and develop proposals to support the sector now falls almost solely with the Department of Trade and Industry, although various other supportive policies are being developed by other government departments. However, the envisaged formal structure through which SMMEs could engage with government has not emerged, and there are plans under way within the Department of Trade and Industry to establish a National Small Business Advisory Council. The main difference between the proposed advisory council and the previous council is that the proposed council will not be a separate institution but rather a body that meets regularly with the Minister on a quarterly basis.

Ntsika was given a wide range of functions, including the coordination and monitoring of the sector and the provision of non-financial services to the sector, assisting SMME service providers, consulting with the Government and service providers and strengthening their capacity to provide support to the sector, as well as undertaking national research on the sector. Its failure, in some respects, to fulfil these functions has now led to it being reinvented as part of the Department of Trade and Industry rather than a separate agency.

Sources: ILO/SEED and Mollentz (2002)

connecting enterprise promotion policies to improvements in the establishment, performance or employment in MSEs. However, small enterprise promotion policies appear to serve a purpose that reaches beyond a direct benefit to the MSE sector and to have the potential to improve the manner in which government as a whole can promote these enterprises. They can improve the coordination of government agencies, create a platform for dialogue between all stakeholders, and facilitate the mobilization of a broader range of resources from civil society and the private sector. The potential of small enterprise promotion policies to contribute to policy reform will be explored in more detail in Chapter 5.

4.1.2 Business laws and regulations

Business laws and regulations are an essential component of the policy and legal environment in which all enterprises operate. They set the rules for commercial transactions and enterprise operations. Business laws and regulations govern business activities, including business registration and reporting requirements, and they also regulate the legal status of an enterprise. In most cases, the requirements for an enterprise to formalize are closely linked to other policy fields.

Regulations and laws governing business give government authorities the necessary information to interact with enterprises, and allow them to restrict or promote the creation of enterprises in certain geographic areas or economic sectors when this is in the public interest. As with most laws, they ascribe rights with responsibilities. They can protect an enterprise from unfair competition, a consumer from unscrupulous business practices, and society at large from unhealthy or environmentally detrimental practices.

Enterprises can choose from a range of legal structures in which to organize their commercial activities. Each of these provides specified rights, responsibilities and liabilities. Typical legal structures used by MSEs include sole proprietorships, partnerships (either registered or unregistered), companies (private forms are mostly used by MSE, because public companies are usually for medium-sized or large enterprises), and cooperative societies. In Pakistan, more than 80 per cent of all enterprises are individual proprietorships. According to the MSE survey data, sole proprietorships and unregistered partnerships are dominant in the other countries as well.[2]

---

[2] In Viet Nam, the majority of MSEs correspond to household enterprises, a special semi-formal status (see Ch. 3).

Box 4.5   Cooperatives as a legal structure for small-scale producers

Cooperatives are "autonomous association[s] of persons united voluntarily to meet their common economic, social and cultural needs and aspirations through a jointly owned and democratically controlled enterprise", according to the Promotion of Cooperatives Recommendation, 2002 (No. 193). They carry out economic activities that support the economic activities of their members, which could include entrepreneurs or workers in the informal economy.

There are various types of cooperatives, including workers' cooperatives, credit cooperatives and consumer cooperatives. Workers' cooperatives, which are also known as production cooperatives, have been particularly successful in activities that lend themselves to joint action, such as catering and restaurants, quarrying and stone-cutting, candle-making and garment manufacture. Craft workers such as tailors, silversmiths, woodcarvers and furniture makers tend to benefit from a looser form of cooperative in which they work as individuals and are credited with the value of the items they make, while the cooperative organizes raw materials, machinery, workshops and markets (ILO, 2002b).

In order to tap the potential of cooperatives to contribute to national development goals such as employment generation and poverty reduction, Recommendation No. 193 points to the importance of a supportive policy and legal framework. The institutional framework should allow for the registration of cooperatives in a rapid, simple and affordable manner, while respecting cooperatives' autonomy. In many countries, reforms of cooperative legislation have been carried out with technical support from the ILO so as to adapt it to the challenges and opportunities generated for cooperatives by economic change and globalization (ILO, 1998).

Cooperatives, although not at the centre of the analysis in this book, are a structure that can offer a series of advantages for small-scale producers (see box 4.5).

We have already noted in Chapter 3 the initiative taken by the Government of Viet Nam to introduce a new kind of legal structure for MSEs known as "household enterprises". This structure promotes ease of entry and a semi-official status, but does not provide all the benefits of a fully registered company or sole proprietor (household enterprises cannot sign contracts, for example). In South Africa, MSEs are able to choose a form of legal structure known as a "closed corporation". The Closed Corporations Act (1984) simplifies registration and compliance requirements for smaller companies with no more than ten directors. It offers limited liability protection and fewer reporting requirements than the Companies Act (1973).

Legal entities designed specifically for MSEs

While business income tax registration is in most cases the first step in setting up a business (see section 4.1.4 below), there are various other obligations of registration or licensing with national and local government authorities. In Chile, Peru and the United Republic of Tanzania, more than three-quarters of micro-enterprises and an even higher share of small enterprises in the MSE survey samples were registered with local authorities. In South Africa, the registration rate was much lower. Viet Nam is an exception, where micro-enterprises are registered with local authorities at a higher rate than small enterprises. This is because household enterprises, of which the majority are micro-enterprises, are obliged to register and obtain the necessary licences for their business with the district People's Committee Business Bureau (table 4.1). As argued in Chapter 3, most MSEs are neither fully formal nor fully informal. Rather, they tend to comply with some of the regulatory requirements while evading others.

Complying with business laws and regulations is a higher burden on MSEs than on larger enterprises

Business laws and regulations affect smaller enterprises differently to larger ones. MSEs suffer most from the difficulties in registering a business. Although all enterprises are affected by the high cost of complying with business laws and regulations and the need to interact with a number of government agencies, this places a relatively higher burden on MSEs than on larger enterprises. For example, while the same monetary cost of registration (such as registration fees, legal fees, stamp duties) may be applied to enterprises of all sizes, this is more difficult to bear for a smaller enterprise that works with less capital and has a lower turnover than a larger enterprise. Likewise, the relative burden of time-consuming procedures is higher for a small enterprise that typically does not have specialized administrative staff available. For many entrepreneurs, time is a more important obstacle than monetary cost. Finally, in some settings, larger enterprises are more likely than smaller ones to have relationships with government officials or the "political clout" to obtain favourable treatment.

This anti-MSE bias in legislation has two dimensions: its structure and its implementation. In the countries under study, many business laws were found to contain a structural bias, in which the particular needs and circumstances of MSEs have been overlooked. Business laws and regulations have either been designed to address the circumstances of larger enterprises – even though the majority of enterprises are either

Table 4.1   Business registration of surveyed MSEs with national and local authorities, 2001 (percentages)

	National authorities		Local authorities	
	Micro	Small	Micro	Small
Chile	67.1	80.6	78.3	84.9
Guinea	20.8	30.8	...	...
Peru	...	...	79.5	96.9
South Africa	...	...	20.5	60.0
Tanzania, United Rep. of	...	...	86.1	94.9
Viet Nam	24.6	56.6	53.8	42.5

Notes: ... not applicable. In Pakistan, business registration of unincorporated enterprises is done through business income tax registration (see table 4.6).

Source: ILO MSE Surveys 2001.

micro or small – or, by treating all enterprise size classes the same, they have placed MSEs at a disadvantage because of these enterprises' resource constraints.

There may be many reasons for a structural anti-MSE bias. In some cases it may be because policy-makers and legislators are unfamiliar with the dynamics of a micro- or small enterprise. The functions, management systems and production cycles of medium-sized and large enterprises are often more commonly understood by government officials – especially by those who have obtained a typical MBA in business or public policy. However, the dynamics of MSEs are different to those of larger enterprises and the effect of laws and regulations can also be different.

A structural MSE bias can also be created because of the competition between MSEs and larger enterprises. Medium-sized and large enterprises, as well as state-owned enterprises, are usually well represented through chambers of commerce, industry associations and other kinds of enterprise formations. They can lobby government for laws and regulations that are friendlier to them and may even be given specific exemptions. Thus, MSEs can suffer a structural bias against them because they are not well organized and thus do not have effective advocates. Large enterprises and corporations can use various channels of political influence, including public relations campaigns highlighting their contribution to national GDP, donations to political parties and participation in elite circles that often sway government decision-making. MSEs, on the other hand, hold very little political power of this kind.

The second kind of bias against MSEs concerns the implementation of business legislation. The mechanisms and institutions designed by government to implement business laws and regulations were found to have a direct effect on MSEs. This effect usually involved increasing costs and complexities for compliance. In some countries, for example, the government authorities that register enterprises are concentrated in the capital or in a handful of administrative capitals. This increases the cost of compliance for enterprises outside these big cities. In the United Republic of Tanzania it is estimated that it is five to ten times more expensive to register a business in the Mwanza region in the north of the country than in the capital Dar es Salaam, when the costs of travel to the capital are included. Likewise, in Guinea enterprises face much higher costs to register when they are located in rural areas.

Overlaps make registration unnecessarily complex for MSEs In some countries, business laws and regulations work in a complementary and coordinated manner; enterprises simultaneously obtain their business registration and their tax registration, or their registration with labour departments. However, in many countries such coordination does not exist. Indeed, it is common to find cases where there are too many laws and regulations that are unclear, overlapping, inconsistent or contradictory. In many countries, enterprises have to interact with a series of government ministries, departments and divisions. In a way, the State requires the enterprises "to compensate for the lack of communication between the various government agencies" (Arroyo and Nebelung, 2002, p. 80).

In the United Republic of Tanzania, the Business Licensing Act (1972) makes it mandatory for all enterprises to obtain a legal document of authorization to do business. Separately, the Business Names (Registration) Ordinance (1958) obliges enterprises to register a business name. Such multiple registration and licensing requirements could be simplified without any negative impact on the Government's legitimate regulation and information requirements.

In Viet Nam the introduction of the new Enterprise Law (2000) significantly reduced the steps that MSEs are required to take in the process of registration. Where once there were 13 steps necessary, there are now only three. In addition, the Enterprise

Law has abolished some 150 sub-licences that were previously in place and has created a simplified and uniform system of registration across the country. Despite this, district-level government authorities have retained powers over business laws and regulations, which has led to unnecessary bureaucratic hurdles in unexpected forms. The report on Viet Nam prepared for this study (Pham, 2002) cites a case in Ninh Thuan Province where an enterprise owner-manager who wishes to purchase a vehicle for business purposes must proceed through ten regulatory steps. These include the requirements to meet directly with the Chief of the Department of Transportation to buy an application form, to seek permission from the District People's Committee, the District Economic Department and the police, and to invite the Department of Transportation to check the proposed place for parking the vehicle.

In some cases, business laws and regulations can lead to harassment by authorities, as many MSEs are unaware of their rights and responsibilities under the government's laws and regulations. The extent of this problem varies across countries; in Chile, for example, the lack of information on laws and regulations seems to be much less of a problem than in other countries. The scope for harassment is greater where business laws give government officials discretionary power to either concede or deny authorization. While licences generally require approval from a government authority, registering does not generally require such an approval. For most economic activities, several studies have recommended replacing licensing requirements with simple registration (for example, Djankov et al., 2000; Rice, 2000).

In sum, deficiencies in the design and implementation of business laws and regulations hinder MSEs either through the costs of compliance or by excluding them from the regulatory framework. Although larger enterprises are also affected, the negative consequences are highest for the smallest enterprises.

Studies to measure the time and costs involved in registering a business have been carried out in many countries, and they have helped to raise public attention around this topic (such as Abuodha and Bowles, 2000a and 2000b; Djankov et al., 2000; OECD, 2001). In some cases, the studies to measure these costs have been related upfront to measures of policy or administrative reform to improve the situation. A recent case

Improved design and implementation of business laws and regulations help MSEs register

Box 4.6   Good practice: Monitoring red tape for reform in Chile

In Chile, the Government started to monitor bureaucratic red tape across the 341 municipalities in the country, while at the same time introducing reforms for improved local implementation of business laws and regulations.

The Ministry of Economy developed a methodology (the "*tramitometro*") to measure the complexity of paperwork required to obtain the municipal permit to run a business. On average, an enterprise took 26.3 days to obtain the licence for industrial activities and 17.3 days for commercial activities. The measurement revealed enormous differences between the 310 city councils that participated in the study. In one municipality, a business could obtain a business licence in only one day. At the other end of the scale, in another municipality the same procedure took 313 days. Some city councils ask for as many as 28 documents in order to endorse the permit. Based on the first measurement in 2000, it is planned to elaborate an improved methodology for a periodical monitoring of progress.

To streamline this procedure, the Chilean Government initiated the Simplification of Paperwork Programme. The operational objective of the programme is to reduce the requirements to a maximum of one week to obtain the permit, no more than six documents to be presented for industries and trade enterprises, one single form to be filled in, and two visits to government agencies.

To achieve these goals, private consultants have been hired to incorporate new management techniques and to re-organize the work in the municipalities. Between 1997 and 2001, around 100 of the 341 municipalities in Chile have benefited from the pro-gramme. The programme resulted in a diminution of the number of documents requested from the entrepreneur (in 71 per cent of cases), the number of persons involved in the licence approval (71 per cent), and the number of visits to different government offices (53 per cent).

Sources: Flores (forthcoming), and http://www.minecon.cl/tramitometro/index.htm.

of good practice comes from Chile, where the delays and procedures to obtain a business permit were compared across municipalities and linked to specific programmes to reduce these delays, as shown in box 4.6.

Reforms of business laws and regulations help MSEs to create more and better employment   Reforms in business laws and regulations can also have a significant positive impact on employment. Simplifying laws and regulations facilitates compliance, and through this can boost both the quantity and quality of jobs. As described previously, the introduction of the new Enterprise Law in Viet Nam has made registration easier. It has also had a significant impact on employment. Before the law was enacted in 2000,

Figure 4.1 Annually registered private enterprises in Viet Nam, 1992–2001

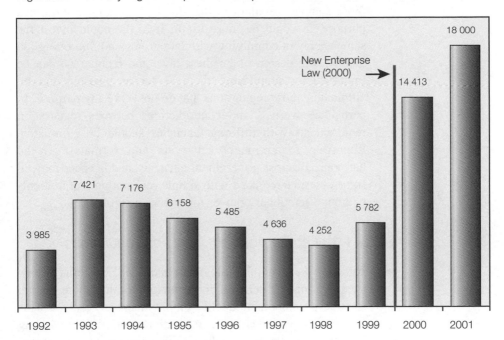

Note: Data for 2001 are estimates. According to data from the Ministry of Finance, by 30 September 2001, 66,071 enterprises were registered under the Enterprise Law and declared tax codes.

Source: Pham (2002).

there were around 5,000 enterprises registered per year; this figure has jumped up to around 15,000 per year since then (figure 4.1). About 70 per cent of these enterprises are truly new, while the others can be attributed to the regularization of previously unregistered enterprises. Given that formal enterprises provide more protected jobs than informal ones, the law has contributed to improved job quality by encouraging the transition from informal to formal. It may also have boosted the volume of employment by increasing the number of new enterprise start-ups.

By contrast, the reforms of business laws and regulations in Peru have not led to measurable improvements in job quality. This may be explained by the dismantling of labour market institutions, which occurred simultaneously with the reforms, as we shall discuss in the following section.

Rather than wasting time and effort in complying with those complex regulations that do not have a clearly defined purpose, it would be more useful if MSEs could invest the same energy in complying with labour law and improving job quality. The design of business laws and regulations can be improved by simplifying them as far as possible and by eliminating those regulations that do not serve any purpose. In particular, overlaps and contradictions between registration requirements with different agencies should be eliminated. Reporting requirements (intervals and formats) can be harmonized across government agencies, and licences may, in some cases, be replaced with simple registration requirements without discretionary power for government officials.

4.1.3 Labour policies, laws and regulations

Although the level of employment in the MSE sector is largely a result of market demand, the regulation of the labour market and the promotion of quality employment are critical. This policy field includes laws, regulations and legally binding collective agreements dealing with employment in MSEs.[3] In this discussion, the main findings from the research deal with labour policies and their coverage and compliance by MSEs; social security coverage; and social dialogue and unionization.

Labour laws and MSEs: Coverage and compliance

Labour laws in many countries exempt MSEs up to a certain size from compliance

Labour laws and regulations affect enterprises of different sizes in different ways. There is an interesting variation across countries in the ways labour issues apply to the MSE sector, as shown in box 4.7. At one extreme, Pakistan exempts all enterprises below a certain size from compliance with all labour laws. At the other end of the spectrum, in Chile and Peru most labour regulations in principle apply to all enterprises, regardless of their size.

Labour laws and regulations can affect job quality in MSEs. Designing and implementing policies that enhance MSE owner-managers' and workers' job quality without

---

[3] In common law countries, court decisions about these texts are also relevant.

Box 4.7	Summary of application of labour policies to MSEs
Chile	Most laws apply to all size classes. Relatively high compliance, although decreasing over the 1990s.
Guinea	Labour laws apply to all enterprise size classes in theory, but not in practice.
Pakistan	Enterprises below ten workers are exempted from labour laws. For some laws the limit has recently been lowered to five workers.
Peru	Most laws apply to all size classes. However, enterprises with fewer than 20 workers are exempted from the regulations governing union membership, mandatory participation in profits, and training levy. Implementation efforts are insufficient.
South Africa	Most labour laws apply to MSEs but compliance is rather low, which may partly be due to high compliance costs. The Employment Equity Act (1998) excludes MSEs, applying only to enterprises with more than 50 workers and above a minimum annual turnover.
Tanzania, United Republic of	Enterprises with fewer than ten workers are excluded from some labour laws. In practice, a low share of MSEs has written work contracts and social security coverage.
Viet Nam	Household enterprises are outside the scope of the labour code and cannot sign work contracts. As a consequence, employment relationships remain informal in this type of enterprise.

Source: Country papers.

creating excessive compliance costs for these enterprises is an important challenge. In many countries, the design of labour legislation has not taken the needs of small enterprises into account, and little systematic knowledge exists in this regard.

At this time it is fair to say that too little is known about just how various elements of labour legislation or of labour market functioning more generally affect SME to allow anyone to design the ideal system from that sector's point of view. What is clear is that the needs of SME are seldom fed articulately into the pool of information on the basis of which judgements are made. (Berry, 1995, p. 15)

General exemptions leave MSE workers unprotected and can create growth traps for enterprises close to the threshold

Most "best practice" statements (OECD, 1999) view labour regulations essentially as restrictions that tend to hamper business development and thus employment creation, but there is little consideration of the actual impact of labour regulations on small enterprise development, or of the potential positive impact of regulations on workers' welfare and labour productivity.

General exemptions of MSEs from labour laws and regulations leave many workers unprotected and thus have a negative impact on job quality. They can also create a growth trap for MSEs by creating incentives for enterprises close to the threshold size either to stop hiring workers or to do so without written contracts.[4] Several ILO studies (for example, ILO, 1997, and Tokman et al., 2001) have argued against a separate labour regulations regime for small enterprises, especially where basic minimum standards and worker rights are concerned. An analysis of labour regulations and minimum wages in 14 Latin American countries suggests that a minimum wage of up to two-thirds of the average wage in enterprises with up to five workers does not have negative consequences in terms of non-compliance and increased informality (ILO, 1997, pp. 42–43).

There are some areas where international labour Conventions allow countries to adopt special provisions for small enterprises, particularly in the areas of employment contracts, social security and collective bargaining. For example, the Termination of Employment Convention, 1982 (No. 158), allows some categories of workers to be excluded from its provisions in the event of special problems arising from the "size or nature" of the enterprise.[5] More generally, the ILO supports the elimination of unnecessary provisions or their replacement by others producing similar results with less bureaucracy and a more flexible application of regulations (von Potobsky, 1992).

---

[4] In addition to the negative consequences for employment creation and employment quality, such exemption may also undermine the incentives for MSEs to upgrade their production and to produce for more demanding markets (Tendler, 2002).

[5] For example, Venezuela and Italy have relaxed the regulation of dismissals in small enterprises (ILO, 2000a, p. 15).

The simplification of labour laws for certain categories of enterprises and workers in the informal economy should not involve any lowering of core labour standards (ILO, 2002b). Exemptions for MSEs should be based on careful analysis to determine whether the costs of certain labour regulations outweigh their benefits for MSEs. South Africa can be mentioned as an example of good practice: special studies were carried out before deciding whether or not to apply the Basic Conditions of Employment Act (1997) to MSEs, as described in box 4.8.

Simplifying compliance and improving implementation can increase the coverage of labour regulations

In Pakistan, the number and complexity of labour regulations has been identified as a major obstacle to compliance. For small enterprises (those with under ten workers are exempt), there are 136 steps required for compliance under the Factories Act (1934). Even laws on related topics that are implemented by the same department are contained in separate legal documents. Enterprises in export processing zones (EPZs), on the other hand, benefit from a one-stop modality whereby all labour laws are implemented in a simplified manner that does not require enterprise owner-managers to deal with individual labour departments. Most enterprises benefiting from this scheme are medium-sized or large, which creates a bias against MSEs. Currently, there is an attempt to

---

Box 4.8   Good practice: Assessing the impact of new labour laws on MSEs

South Africa provides a good example of the assessment of the impact of new labour laws on MSEs before their implementation. A study commissioned by the South African enterprise promotion agency Ntsika (Ntsika, 1998) quantifies the potential impact of the introduction of a new Basic Conditions of Employment Act (1997) on MSEs. This assessment was used as an input in the discussion on whether or not to exempt small enterprises from some of the regulations in the Act. The study comes up with cost estimations for complying with the new regulations. The methodology included telephone surveys designed to capture the current degree of compliance with legal regulations and binding collective agreements.

The study concludes that no general exemptions for small enterprises are necessary, but points to some economic sectors where the additional cost might hamper enterprise development and employment creation, and therefore recommends a more flexible treatment for those sectors.

Source: ILO/SEED based on Ntsika (1998).

---

reduce the number of laws in the package of labour laws from 27 to six. This would facilitate compliance without any negative side effect on workers' rights and job quality.

In some countries, labour laws are badly outdated. This risks making legislation seem irrelevant, and can undermine the system's credibility. In the United Republic of Tanzania, for example, some regulations date from the 1940s and 1950s, without the amounts for the assessment of wages or penalties ever being updated to compensate for inflation (Tibandebage et al., 2003).

Compliance will not automatically increase with the liberalization of labour laws. In Peru, the share of informal employment (without written contracts and without social security coverage) actually increased during the 1990s, despite the liberalization of labour laws. The reason for this lies in the weakness of the labour market institutions dismantled in parallel with the liberalization efforts. The number of staff members in the Ministry of Labour was cut from around 1,000 in 1990 to 200 in 2001, reducing drastically the Ministry's capacity to monitor the enforcement of labour laws. In fact, in Peru there appears to be a clear correlation between the likelihood of an enterprise to be inspected and the degree of compliance with laws and regulations (Chacaltana, 2001).

Social security coverage for MSEs

Social security coverage is low (and even declining) for MSE owner-managers and workers in most countries

The quality of life of MSE owner-managers and workers can be greatly enhanced by providing them with social security systems, notably health insurance and pension schemes.[6] While social security contributions represent a cost that enterprises have to bear, social security can also have the effect of raising labour productivity by maintaining workers in good health and easing the departure of older workers from the labour force (ILO, 2001b). However, participation by micro-enterprises in social protection schemes has been found to be low in all seven countries. As table 4.2 demonstrates, in most countries even the majority of small enterprises (ten to 49 workers) remain outside the social security system.

---

[6] The Job Creation in Small and Medium-Sized Enterprises Recommendation, 1998 (No. 189), therefore recommends the review of social and labour legislation to ensure that social protection extends to workers in small enterprises.

Table 4.2   Surveyed MSEs providing social security coverage, 2001 (percentages)

	Pension or old age insurance		Health insurance	
	Micro-enterprises (2–9 workers)	Small enterprises (10–49 workers)	Micro-enterprises (2–9 workers)	Small enterprises (10-49 workers)
Chile	22.2	46.8	25.5	56.8
Guinea	1.5	5.8	1.5	9.6
Pakistan	1.2	14.6	..	..
Peru	19.8	66.8	27.5	75.5
South Africa	4.0	26.7	13.3	33.3
Tanzania, United Rep. of	3.0	29.3	10.4	52.5
Viet Nam	12.6	38.9	13.1	27.4

Notes: .. not available. Data refer to answers provided by enterprise owner-managers. A positive answer does not necessarily imply social security for the entire workforce in that enterprise. The coverage measured as a share of employment is therefore likely to be lower. However, in Chile, contributions for the pension scheme and the health insurance are paid entirely by the employees, which may have led to MSE owner-managers not mentioning social security as a benefit. For Pakistan, the question refers to "pension/insurance scheme" together.

Source: ILO MSE Surveys 2001.

State-supported social security systems have been experiencing financial pressures in many countries. In some cases, this is because of efforts to reduce government bureaucracy and expenditure; in other cases, it is a result of the inefficiencies of pension funds. New community-based approaches to social security have emerged in some countries in an attempt to redress the declining participation levels and to extend the benefits of social security to vulnerable groups. There are a number of reasons for this, including the design and administration of social security schemes, which seem to fit the needs of large enterprises better than those of MSEs. In addition, MSE workers and employers do not always appreciate the value of being covered by the social security system, either because the quality of the benefits is perceived to be low, or because the emphasis is on the immediate short-term perspective.

In Viet Nam, the compulsory system of social insurance only applies to enterprises that employ ten or more workers. In Pakistan, too, enterprises with fewer than ten workers used to be exempted from affiliating themselves to the social security system, although recently enterprises with five to nine workers have been added to the compulsory coverage of the social security system. However, this measure can only be successful if at the same time institutional capacities are strengthened to ensure implementation. In fact, according to the MSE survey, only a minority of enterprises in Pakistan with ten to 49 workers were registered with the Employees' Social Security Institution (15 per cent) and the Employees' Old Age Benefit Institution (25 per cent) in 2001.

When statutory social insurance is extended to smaller enterprises, each new employer has to be identified, registered, educated and persuaded to comply with all the rules of the scheme in so far as they relate to the registration of existing and new employees and to the method and payment of contributions (Jenkins, 1993). Successful efforts to extend and improve social security coverage have been made in a number of countries (Ginneken, 2003), but unfortunately other countries have experienced a decline in coverage among MSEs. The data available for Pakistan, for example, show that the number of insured workers in the Employees' Social Security Institution dropped by 1.2 per cent between 1996 and 1999, while the labour force increased by 9 per cent over the same period. Both in Peru and in Chile, social security coverage slightly decreased during the 1990s, but the decline was most pronounced in MSEs, as table 4.3 illustrates. In Chile, the coverage among salaried workers in micro-enterprises declined from 46.8 per cent to 39.7 per cent, while in large enterprises coverage remained almost stable. In Peru, coverage declined from 25.2 to 10.4 per cent in micro-enterprises, while it increased in large enterprises.

Innovative approaches are needed to improve social protection   It is essential to improve the governance, financing and administration of social security schemes in order to increase social protection for MSE owner-managers and workers. This includes the simplification of overlapping schemes and administrative procedures. For example, in Pakistan employers are required to pay seven different social security contributions. Reducing the number of contributions would make the system more "MSE-friendly".

The Social Security (Minimum Standards) Convention, 1952 (No. 102), was one of the first international labour Conventions that permitted a country to exclude small enterprises (employing fewer than 20 workers) in the

Table 4.3   Social security coverage (pension schemes) by enterprise size, Chile and
            Peru, 1990 and 2000 (percentages)

Enterprise size	Chile		Peru	
	1990	2000	1990	2000
Micro (1–9 workers)	46.8	39.7	25.2	10.4
Small (10–49)	86.1	82.1	60.0	41.4
Medium-sized (50–199)	91.2	88.7	72.6	67.5
Large (200 and more)	93.3	91.9	81.4	84.6

Notes: Coverage is defined as the share of salaried workers contributing to a pension scheme. Data for Peru refer to Lima and exclude public sector workers. These household survey data are not directly comparable to the MSE survey data presented in table 4.2.

Sources: ILO/SEED based on data from Encuesta de caracterización socioeconómica nacional (CASEN) and Chacaltana (2001).

calculation of contributions and beneficiaries for some benefits (von Potobsky, 1992). The current approach of the ILO to increasing the coverage of social security combines the broadening of existing social security systems with micro-insurance schemes as a first step in responding to people's urgent need for improved access to health care. Such micro-insurance schemes are often based within groups which are already organized to provide micro-credit facilities to their members. As an extension of their services, such groups may decide to cover health risks among their members (ILO, 2000b, p. 87). Whenever possible, efforts should be made to link self-help or micro-insurance schemes with formal social security systems. Policies and initiatives on the extension of coverage should be taken within the context of an integrated national social security strategy.

In some of the countries under study, specific social protection schemes for micro-enterprises have been established to compensate for the lack of formal protection. These informal schemes include rotating savings and credit schemes, savings and credit cooperatives, NGOs, self-help organizations and producer cooperatives. For example, in the United Republic of Tanzania, the most common form of informal protection against loss of income in the Dar es Salaam Informal Sector Survey was the rotating and savings and credit scheme known as Upatu. However, the membership in such organizations tends to be low compared to the total number of micro-enterprises (Tibandebage et al., 2003).

So far, micro-insurance schemes in most countries have reached only a very small proportion of the poor and of workers in the informal economy. Such schemes are not available in most areas, and when they are, the poor (especially women) have little or no knowledge about them.

Social dialogue and unionization

One of the central findings of this research project across the seven countries has been the insufficient representation of the MSE sector in policy-making processes. Social dialogue can be an important tool to incorporate MSE concerns into economic policy-making, as well as to bring about a fair balance between the interests of MSE owner-managers and workers. However, MSEs and their workers are difficult to organize because of the high number of units, their relative isolation and the fragile legal status of many small enterprises.

In many countries, unionization and collective bargaining are legally linked to a certain minimum size of the enterprise (von Potobsky, 1992; Vega, 1996). Workers in enterprises below this minimum size can only be covered by virtue of sectoral or national unions and collective agreements.[7]

Trade union membership in MSEs is low In all countries studied, trade union membership and coverage of collective bargaining in MSEs are low. In South Africa, for example, the share of enterprises with trade unions or collective bargaining rises dramatically with enterprise size. Among micro-enterprises, trade union coverage is around 13 per cent and collective bargaining 10 per cent, while among enterprises with between 50 and 99 employees these rates rise to 93 per cent and 82 per cent, as table 4.4 illustrates. In the United Republic of Tanzania, the percentage of enterprises unionized jumps from 12 per cent for micro-enterprises and 33 per cent for small to 96 per cent for large (see table 2.3 in Chapter 2). The private sector unionization rate in Peru in 1999 was 20 per cent of salaried workers in large enterprises, but only 3 per cent in small enterprises. Similarly, a study in Chile found that only 4 per cent of the micro-enterprises and 10 per cent of the small

---

[7] This limitation to unionization would appear to be problematic in the context of the Freedom of Association and Protection of the Right to Organize Convention, 1948 (No. 87). In fact, the ILO Committee of Freedom of Association has repeatedly raised concerns about the exclusion of workers in micro-enterprises from the right to join a trade union (Schlyter, 2002, pp. 8–9).

Table 4.4   Share of enterprises with trade unions and collective bargaining, by enterprise size, South Africa, 1999 (percentages)

No. of employees	Trade union	Collective bargaining
1 to 5	13	10
6 to 20	27	28
21 to 49	54	58
50 to 99	93	82
100 to 199	95	86
200 or more	99	97

Note: The figures are based on surveys of 792 MSEs (1 to 49 employees) in various economic sectors, and 325 manufacturing enterprises with 50 or more employees.

Sources: Chandra et al. (2001a and 2001b).

enterprises had a trade union, while this share was 38 per cent for medium-sized enterprises and 57 per cent for large (Espinosa et al., 2000). Likewise, the coverage of collective bargaining in Chile is close to zero in micro-enterprises and only 2 per cent in small enterprises, compared to 29 per cent in large enterprises.[8]

In addition to the weakness of trade unions and the low coverage of collective bargaining, representative bodies within the enterprise, such as work councils, are also much weaker in small enterprises than in larger ones. This is due to legal restrictions in national legislations and the relatively higher operational cost of staff representation in small enterprises (von Potobsky, 1992).

MSE owner-managers can affiliate themselves with employers' associations, chambers of commerce or small enterprise associations. In some countries, many MSEs are affiliated with informal sector associations or with some type of social organization.[9] According to the MSE surveys, only 8 to 37 per cent of micro-enterprise owner-managers are affiliated with employers' associations, chambers of commerce or small

[8] Authors' calculations based on data from CASEN 1998 and Dirección del Trabajo (2000a). Coverage is defined here as the number of workers covered by collective bargaining as a share of total salaried employment. These data are therefore not directly comparable to the data on collective bargaining for South Africa, which refer to the share of enterprises and are based on sample surveys for certain economic sectors.

[9] The *jua kali* associations in Kenya are an example of informal sector associations. These associations allow operators in the informal economy to take joint action to respond to the scarcity of raw materials, licensing requirements, the incidence of police harassment and the need for advocacy. According to a recent study, 30 per cent of sample MSEs were *jua kali* members, and almost 90 per cent were member of some business or social association (McCormick et al., 2001).

Table 4.5   Membership of surveyed MSEs with private sector organizations, 2001
(percentages)

	Chamber of commerce		Business association		Employers' organization		Any private sector organization	
	Micro	Small	Micro	Small	Micro	Small	Micro	Small
Chile	..	..	..	..	..	..	7.5	12.9
Guinea	16.5	28.8	25.4	40.4	10.4	11.5	36.9	63.5
Pakistan	7.1	32.9	10.1	44.5	2.4	23.2	13.6	58.5
Peru	4.0	20.9	6.9	13.3	0.6	3.6	10.7	31.6
South Africa	..	..	33.7	53.3	3.2	16.7	34.5	56.7
Tanzania, United Rep. of	8.0	17.2	9.5	22.2	1.5	13.1	16.9	39.4
Viet Nam	6.5	23.0	3.0	14.2	3.5	5.3	10.1	36.3

Notes: .. not available. In the Chilean questionnaire, the question was not disaggregated by type of private sector organization.

Source: ILO MSE Surveys 2001.

enterprise associations. Among the small enterprises, however, this share is considerably higher, ranging from 13 per cent in Chile to 64 per cent in Guinea (table 4.5).

Closing the "representational gap" (ILO, 2002b) and increasing the role of MSE owner-managers and workers in social dialogue is an important means to improving their social and economic situation, both within the workplace and in a larger national context. Employers' and workers' organizations play a critical role in extending membership and services to MSEs, as well as in encouraging and supporting the creation of new member-based, accessible, transparent, accountable and democratically managed representative organizations (ILO, 2002a). The role of private sector associations in facilitating MSEs' access to resources, to training or to incentive schemes is crucial because, unlike large enterprises, these enterprises are generally too small to organize access individually. Effective bodies of MSE representation can make the voice of this category of enterprises heard in policy-making arenas to ensure that the impact of new laws and regulations on the MSE sector is taken into account. MSE associations can also help develop the market for business development services for MSEs.

Mechanisms of implementation

In most countries, governments give less attention to the implementation of labour standards through laws, social security coverage, social dialogue and unionization than to compliance with tax obligations and business regulations.[10] Implementation mechanisms and institutions in the field of labour policies are either very weak, or they rely on labour inspections as the sole means of monitoring compliance. Other methods, such as self-reporting or commissioning business associations for this purpose, are rarely used.

While governments need to be realistic about the capacity of MSEs to comply with labour regulations, there should be no general exemptions from basic labour norms. Simplifying overly complex regulations, making specific norms more flexible based on a careful assessment, and improving the mechanisms of implementation beyond labour inspections are better means to meet the twin objectives of employment creation and job quality.

4.1.4 Taxation policies, laws and regulations

This policy field includes different types of taxes, such as income and company taxes, profit taxes, value added tax (VAT), sales taxes and capital taxes, as well as tax incentive schemes and tax rebates. Driven by the need to balance state budgets, many governments in developing countries have taken measures to broaden their tax base. As a result, MSEs are now often incorporated into the tax net, as can be seen in table 4.6. In all countries, more than three-quarters of small urban enterprises in the survey sample were registered for business income tax purposes. Among the urban micro-enterprises in all countries except South Africa, more than half of the sample enterprises are registered. In Peru, tax registration was virtually universal among urban MSEs, reflecting the fact that recent tax reforms have simplified registration (see box 5.4 in Chapter 5, p. 141).

Most MSEs have to pay taxes

Many MSEs are obliged to pay taxes even when they are not registered. The risk for such enterprises is that they are in a situation where they face some of the costs of regulations, without being able to reap the potential benefits of formalization. For example, in Viet Nam, household

---

[10] In this context, the Labour Administration Convention, 1978 (No. 150), states that countries should make efforts to incorporate informal sector operators, by gradual stages if necessary, into the scope of labour administration.

Table 4.6   Business income tax registration of surveyed MSEs by size and location, 2001

	Urban		Rural	
	Micro	Small	Micro	Small
Chile	85.7	91.6	82.1	85.0
Guinea	78.2	67.6	63.5	73.3
Pakistan	54.8	80.3	36.5	46.8
Peru	85.5	99.5	68.8	100.0
South Africa	26.9	76.9	17.1	50.0
Tanzania, United Rep. of	70.7	87.8	38.9	52.9
Viet Nam	55.4	87.9	43.5	70.2

Source: ILO MSE Surveys 2001.

enterprises pay taxes, although they do not benefit from a fully formal status.

On the other hand, the smallest enterprises are often exempt from some taxes or can avoid paying by concealing their incomes. One indicator for this is the relatively high share of micro-enterprises not registered with any tax authority. This is especially the case in South Africa. Even though enterprises sometimes have to pay taxes whether registered or not, some micro-enterprises manage to operate without being detected by tax authorities. In other cases, MSEs can evade taxes, even though they may be registered with tax authorities. However, according to the MSE survey data, tax authorities inspect MSEs more frequently than any other government agency. Moreover, as analysed in Chapter 3, evading government regulations can have other costs for MSEs, such as the risk of persecution and harassment or the lack of access to resources and markets. Finally, the threat of high taxes may keep growth-oriented enterprises from growing, as this would increase their visibility.

As with other policy fields, there are two sides to taxation policy that affect MSEs. First is the design of the taxation system and the structural biases against MSEs. The second concerns the manner in which taxation policies are applied. Here there is a range of institutional and procedural arrangements that can impede the operations of MSEs and which are biased in favour of larger enterprises.

Anti-MSE biases in the design of tax systems

The design of certain systems of taxation is often biased in favour of large enterprises. Structural biases in the seven countries under study arose as a result of three main issues. The first issue is tax exemptions for large enterprises. Large enterprises obtain exemptions or incentives that are unavailable to MSEs, comparatively reducing the operating costs for the large enterprises and thus distorting the market-place. For example, in Viet Nam, state-owned enterprises receive a number of exemptions and benefits that are not available to private sector enterprises. Other tax incentives in Viet Nam are oriented towards enterprises that create a lot of employment. However, due to unclear guidelines for implementation, cumbersome and unrealistic procedures, these policies have a limited impact on the employment patterns in MSEs. Similarly, in the United Republic of Tanzania, tax holidays are available for large enterprises, but not for smaller ones.

Tax exemptions are for large enterprises

These biases can have a direct negative impact on small enterprises, when subsidies are channelled towards large-scale producers of goods that compete directly with small-scale production (Steel and Takagi, 1983). In many cases, those dynamic small enterprises that are formalizing themselves and creating new employment opportunities may be penalized by the tax system because they can neither hide nor obtain benefits from incentive schemes biased towards large enterprises.

The second factor found to work against MSEs is the complexity of taxation. The most common experience among MSEs is the complexity of taxes they are required to pay. In some countries, MSEs are liable for a myriad of taxes, levies and duties. In the United Republic of Tanzania, there are 26 different types of taxes alongside a plethora of local licences, permits, duties and levies, which are more numerous than in most other countries. The study conducted for Viet Nam indicates that "only the tax officers understand the taxes to be paid" (Pham, 2002). In Pakistan, too, the tax system is very complex. There is a simplified self-assessment scheme for some types of MSEs, but this forces enterprises to increase their tax base by 10 per cent each year. In Peru and Chile, by contrast, the tax systems are comparatively simple, and in Peru in particular the tax system has been considerably simplified over

The complexity of tax regulations affects MSEs more than larger enterprises

the 1990s. As a result, even micro-enterprises are generally registered with tax authorities (see table 4.6), although they may not always pay their tax obligations entirely.

Sometimes, tax rates are too high for MSEs

The third structural bias found in many tax systems concerns the rates of taxation. In some countries, tax rates are simply too high for MSEs. Taxes in Viet Nam, for example, were reported to be a heavy burden on MSEs. In other cases, small enterprises may pay no or few taxes, either because they are formally exempted or because they evade taxes. In Pakistan and Peru, MSEs below a certain level of income are exempted from paying taxes or can operate under tax regimes with lower tax rates.

The most common taxes found to apply to MSEs are VAT, income and company tax. However, in some countries other kinds of taxation prove to have unfavourably high rates for MSEs. In the United Republic of Tanzania, for example, MSEs are taxed according to their turnover. While this might initially appear to suit smaller enterprises – because they are more likely to have a lower turnover than large enterprises – its effect is to introduce a bias against MSEs, because MSEs tend to have a lower degree of vertical integration than larger enterprises.[11] Local taxes in Guinea are charged according to a scale with a high minimum amount (FG25,000) and a relatively low maximum (FG70,000). This means that local taxes are dissuasive for the smallest enterprises, while they are relatively low for the largest enterprises. Finally, taxes that are charged as lump sum payments (including licence and registration fees) are biased against the smallest enterprises if these firms are not exempted.

Anti-MSE biases in tax enforcement

Many problems for MSEs in complying with tax obligations arise from the administration of tax laws and regulations. In Viet Nam and the United Republic of Tanzania, there are a number of "hidden costs" to tax compliance for MSEs, such as

---

[11] The term "vertical integration" refers to the integration of operations along the chain of production and commercialization in one single enterprise. The higher the degree of vertical integration, the lower the number of enterprises involved. When each transaction is taxed on the total value (instead of value added), enterprises with a lower degree of vertical integration pay more taxes. These are usually smaller enterprises.

time taken to complete tax forms, travel time and costs for rural-based enterprises. In Chile, the time needed to register and fill in tax declarations was identified as the main problem in complying.

The procedural biases against MSEs in the taxation field were often found to stem from four kinds of problems in the following institutional and procedural arrangements. The first of these was the large number of institutions that applied a tax to MSEs. Along with the problem of complex taxation systems, identified above, these taxes are often administered by too many institutions. In addition to a central tax authority, MSEs may be required to pay land and service taxes to a local authority, and district or provincial taxes to a district or provincial authority, as well as a range of other licensing taxes (such as bed tax for those in the tourism industry). This was found in Viet Nam, for example, where large discrepancies in taxation exist among districts within a province or among industries. Thus, streamlining these taxes and consolidating the number of institutions involved in the administration of taxation can be very beneficial.

Too many institutions are enforcing taxes

The second problem that was found to lead to an anti-MSE bias in tax enforcement concerns the discretion and lack of transparency applied to taxation. Taxation systems with a high degree of discretion in the administration of taxes, such as those reported in the United Republic of Tanzania, have been found to lead to corruption and have a negative effect on the operations of MSEs. This has contributed to many MSEs opting to remain informal and avoid taxation assessments altogether. In Pakistan, the harassment and time loss rather than monetary cost are the main reasons MSEs choose not to register with tax authorities.

Discretion and lack of transparency are problems

The lack of reporting on the use of taxation revenues was also found to be an issue. In many cases, MSEs see little return for their payments. They may pay their taxes regularly, but find that their electricity or water supplies remain insufficient. The collection of taxes implies that government will use these funds to provide infrastructure and services that MSEs can benefit from as a whole. However, this is a tenuous relationship in many instances. Thus, governments can inform the MSE sector about its use of tax revenues in order to build confidence and promote compliance.

There is often a lack of information on the use of taxes

Delays in rebates and rulings affect MSEs

Finally, delays in receiving rebates and rulings can have a negative effect on MSEs. Many MSEs face a hidden cost in taxation brought about by delays in the time taken to receive rebates or other kinds of tax rulings. In Viet Nam, for example, MSEs have reported long waiting periods for VAT refunds and delays by taxation authorities in the issuing of certificates for taxation incentives.

Although MSEs are often thought to be outside the tax net, this idea does not correspond to reality. Most MSEs pay taxes in one form or another. In fact, tax regulations are the regulations that are most rigorously enforced on MSEs. Given the fragility of many MSEs, they are strongly affected by the complexities of most tax systems and the risk of being harassed by tax officials.

4.1.5 Trade policies

Trade policies exert an influence on MSEs because they have an effect on access to, and prices of, imported material inputs, as well as on the price of the enterprise's final products and the possible access to export markets. The field of trade policy includes limitations on the quantity of imports (such as import quotas, import licences) and taxes that make imports more expensive (such as import tariffs), as well as taxes on and incentives for exports.

Export markets have potential for employment creation and poverty reduction

Several studies have recognized the potential of linking low-income producers of artisan items to world markets as a strategy for poverty reduction (Berry, 1997). The results of the MSE surveys show that those enterprises that managed to export their products are more likely over time to expand and create employment than similar enterprises limited to local markets (Christensen and Goedhuys, forthcoming; see also table A.8 in the Annex). However, as a result of weaknesses in the MSEs themselves as well as in trade policies, few MSEs benefit directly from international trade. Most enterprises cover mainly domestic markets, as table 4.7 shows, with a very low percentage exporting their products.

Most developing countries relied on import-substitution strategies to foster industrialization up until around the 1980s. Such import-substitution schemes were generally biased against MSEs because imported inputs were licensed or directly allocated by governments, which favoured large

Table 4.7   Main markets for surveyed MSEs, 2001 (mentions in percentages)

	Local	Regional/national	Export
Chile	53.2	44.1	2.7
Guinea	42.9	52.9	4.2
Pakistan	75.5	20.2	4.2
Peru	77.5	19.4	3.1
South Africa	67.4	31.5	1.1
Tanzania, United Rep. of	34.4	59.5	6.0
Viet Nam	43.3	46.2	10.6

Source: ILO MSE Surveys 2001.

enterprises more likely to gain access to import quotas. Imports of new capital equipment were often given favourable tariff and quota treatment to foster the domestic production of consumer goods, but small enterprise imports of capital equipment often could not benefit from these incentives. This is because small enterprises tend to import either cheaper second-hand machinery which is not covered by these benefits, or types of simple machinery classified as final consumer goods (for example, sewing machines) with less favourable treatment. Furthermore, large enterprises are often granted industrial investment incentives that enable them to import their capital goods duty-free for a certain time (Haggblade et al., 1990; Berry, 1995).

In many countries, trade liberalization has been a key policy reform in developing countries over the last decades. Export and import licences have been abolished, import quotas have been replaced by import tariffs, and tariff rates have been gradually lowered to open to international trade. In the United Republic of Tanzania, for example, the maximum rate of import tariffs has been reduced from more than 50 per cent in the 1980s to 40 per cent in 1995 and 25 per cent in 1999. Recent policy declarations have provided for a further reduction of tariff rates. In Guinea, trade licences were abolished, although import tariffs were recently raised to increase the revenues for the state budget.

Trade liberalization has diminished the inherent bias against MSEs in most import-substitution regimes

Import tariffs, as opposed to import quotas or other non-tariff barriers, were not found to have a differential impact on small compared to large enterprises, as their application is uniform. In principle, therefore, the phasing out of non-tariff import barriers in the context of trade liberalization policies in many developing countries should give MSEs a more favourable environment. However, even import tariffs can be biased against small enterprises when economic sectors dominated by large enterprises are more protected than those sectors characterized by a strong presence of small enterprises (Osmani, 1995; Bagachwa, 1996).

New policies have often been designed in a way that makes it impossible for MSEs to benefit

New export incentives sometimes repeat the experience of discrimination against MSEs by establishing minimum export volumes for the access to incentive schemes. These are often too high for MSEs to benefit from. The policy environment is also an obstacle for potential exporters in Viet Nam, where the legal status of household enterprises does not allow them to export directly.[12]

While in several countries certain incentives are available that aim to foster the development of export sectors across all enterprise size classes, the benefits of these are only available to direct exporters. Cumbersome regulations and procedures often force MSEs to commission larger enterprises or traders for exporting, while the MSEs perform the role of providers (what may be called "indirect exporters"). In Pakistan, the Central Board of Revenue issued more than 25 Statutory Regulatory Orders concerning exportation in one year. This makes it unnecessarily difficult to keep up with the latest trade regulations. Thus, MSEs in Pakistan rarely benefit from the existing export incentive schemes. On the other hand, some countries, such as Chile and Peru, have specific programmes to encourage MSE exports, but their coverage is relatively low.

The process of policy-making in the field of trade policies is often biased against MSEs. In Pakistan, for example, key industry and trade associations are often consulted when decisions about trade policies are made. However, these associations are dominated by large-scale enterprises. The

---

[12] Until 1998, Vietnamese enterprises wishing to engage in export–import activities were required to have a legal capital above US$200,000 in order to obtain an export licence. MSEs were thus excluded from direct exports. The abolition of export licence requirements in 1998 allowed every formally registered enterprise to participate directly in foreign trade.

industry associations, which have a more significant representation of MSEs, do not participate in these consultations or in other decision-making processes.

Although trade liberalization and greater access to the world economy can open up markets for enterprises of all sizes, it also brings greater competition. While large and small enterprises are equally subjected to this competition, their ability to respond to these changes can vary. As many small enterprises do not have the professional management and resources to adapt to the more competitive environment, in the short term this may not be in their interest. Moreover, given the traditionally low import content of small enterprise production, MSEs take little advantage from the cheaper imported inputs that the globalized economy offers (ILO, 1996). On the other hand, small enterprises can be more flexible to fluctuations in demand, while large enterprises often have to cut costs by downsizing and shedding staff, often resulting in an increase in the employment share of MSEs (Cook and Nixson, 2000, p. 8). In order for MSEs to tap the full benefits of international trade, policy-makers should consider the likely impact of trade liberalization by enterprise size and pay special attention to the policy obstacles that MSEs face in international markets.

4.1.6 Finance and credit policies, laws and regulations

Our main interest in the field of finance policies is in public policy, legal and regulatory instruments that affect MSEs' access to capital, including regulations that determine the conditions for financial institutions to give credit (prudential regulations) and government incentives for finance providers to improve their coverage of MSEs. Specific finance programmes run by non-governmental or community organizations are not examined, as our focus is on the role that public policy plays in the flow of finance to the MSE sector.

Despite the problems identified in the policy environment of the countries under study, many MSEs do have links to the financial system. One indicator of this is the existence of bank accounts. In all seven countries, the majority of small enterprises have a bank account. Among the micro-enterprises,

Many MSEs have links to the banking system and apply for credit

Figure 4.2 Existence of bank account among surveyed MSEs, 2001 (percentages)

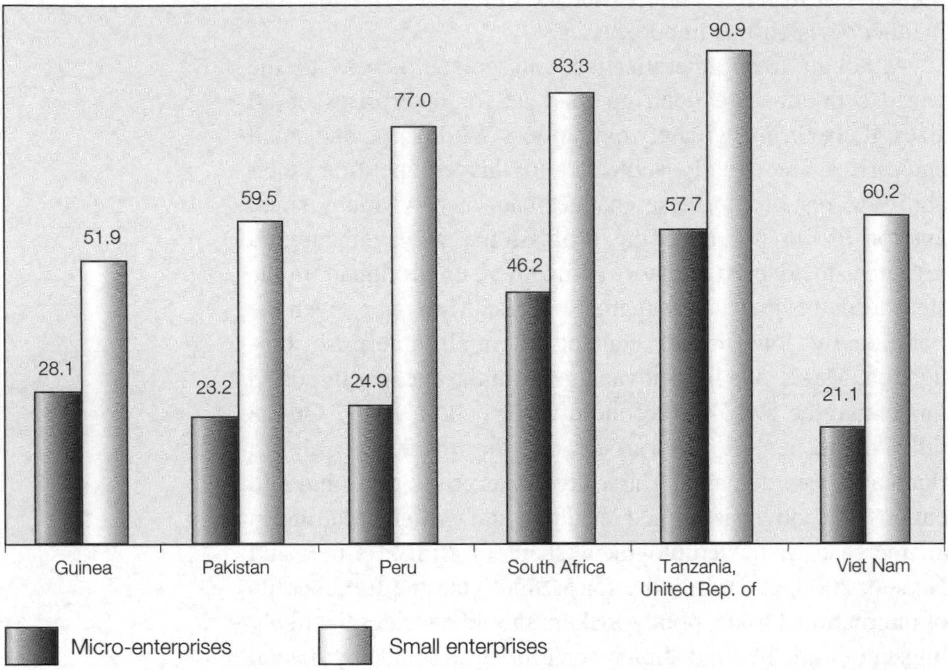

Note: Survey data for Chile are not available, but various studies demonstrate that most MSEs in Chile have business bank accounts (Held, 1999; Inversiones y Gestión Ltda., 2002).

Source: ILO MSE Surveys 2001.

this share ranges from 21 per cent in Viet Nam to 58 per cent in the United Republic of Tanzania, as illustrated in figure 4.2.

Access to finance is among the four most-mentioned factors having a positive impact on employment creation, according to the MSE surveys. Likewise, the lack of finance was cited among the key factors that led enterprises to reduce the size of their workforce. In most countries, around half of the enterprises in the survey samples attempted to obtain formal credit during the period 1999 to 2001, with lower shares in Pakistan and the United Republic of Tanzania. Not all enterprises succeeded. In Guinea, only one-third of the enterprises that attempted to obtain credit were granted it, while in the other countries this share fluctuated between 50 and 80 per cent.

Among the seven countries under study, Chile is the country with the highest rate of access to formal credit for MSEs, while

Figure 4.3 Formal credit access during 1999 to 2001 in surveyed MSEs (percentages)

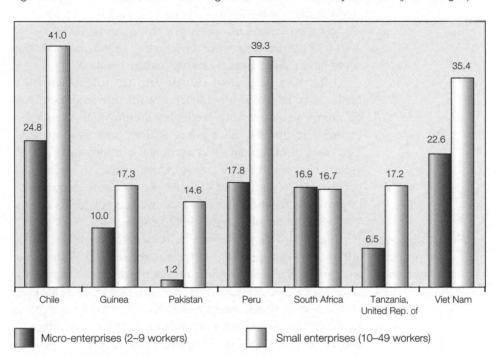

Micro-enterprises (2–9 workers)   Small enterprises (10–49 workers)

Note: Formal credit refers to business loans from a private or public bank, a government credit fund or an international project.

Source: ILO MSE Surveys 2001.

Guinea, Pakistan and the United Republic of Tanzania have the lowest. As figure 4.3 shows, in Chile 41 per cent of small enterprises and 25 per cent of micro-enterprises in the MSE survey sample obtained credit during the period 1999 to 2001. These relatively high shares are especially remarkable as the economic slowdown during this period had reduced MSEs' access to credit compared to the previous period (see box 4.9). In Chile and Guinea, formal credit access was considerably lower for women-owned enterprises than for male-owned enterprises, while in the other countries it was slightly higher for women-owned enterprises.

Business start-ups rarely have access to formal credit. While the MSE surveys included only MSEs with at least two workers that had been operating for at least two years, finance is especially scarce for enterprise start-ups. For example, only 3 per cent of the

Business start-ups rarely have access to formal credit

sample enterprises in Pakistan were financed through formal credit at start-up. It is likely that many job creation opportunities are lost due to a lack of access to starting capital (D.M. Gross, 2001). Therefore, improving the policies of financial mediation could have a direct impact on employment creation.

Difficulties with credit access are due to problems that MSEs have in providing collateral or reliable records of past economic activity, and to the higher administrative costs that financial institutions have when dealing with low amounts. The costs of uncertainty and asymmetric information are too great to be absorbed by private agents such as lenders and borrowers. A variety of policies is therefore required to improve the functioning of finance markets for MSEs (Berry, 1995; Snodgrass and Biggs, 1996; D.M. Gross, 2001).

Reducing costs for financial intermediaries can help MSEs access credit

Collateral deficiencies are an important constraint, but in different ways depending on the enterprise size. With micro-enterprises, the main problem for intermediaries is usually the absence of assets that these enterprises can pledge, while the main problem with small enterprises is the high cost involved in establishing and processing the value of the collateral (Balkenhol and Schütte, 2001). Providing collateral assets is especially difficult in countries where the property market is not fully developed, such as in Viet Nam; in practice, household enterprises in Viet Nam are largely blocked from access to formal credit. Policy reforms need to consider ways to reduce these costs for financial institutions and to make it easier for MSEs to use collateral substitutes.

Credit registries can help to improve access to credit for MSEs. These registries collect information on payment histories to improve information flows on small borrowers and allow potential borrowers to use their good reputation to secure finance, thus reducing expense and risk for lenders (World Bank, 2002). By extending funds to financial institutions that have loan schemes for MSEs, government can also provide motivation to reach out to these enterprises. Another important incentive to potential lenders is competition in the banking system: this may be one of the explanations for the relatively high rates of credit access in Chile and Peru.

The main policy challenge in this field is to improve MSE access to credit by establishing mechanisms to help small enterprises access credit at market rates, rather than providing cheap credit to a small number of enterprises. However, most countries have addressed the challenge of MSE finance by setting up new institutions and programmes that have a limited outreach or are poorly focused.

In Pakistan, the Small Business Finance Corporation provides financial assistance to MSEs on soft terms, but only a small share of the funds disbursed actually reaches the target group. The Government of South Africa has established Khula Enterprise Finance Ltd as a parastatal agency focused on the provision of micro-finance to MSEs. In Viet Nam, a number of special funds have been established to address the financial needs of MSEs. These include the Fund for Hunger Eradication and Poverty Alleviation Programme, the Job Creation Fund, the Fund for German-Vietnamese Returnees' Programme, the EU Small and Medium Enterprises Development Fund, and the Supporting Development Fund. Many of these funds have tapped into the financial resources of donor agencies and have created little or no change in the policy framework.

Most countries rely on a programme approach with limited outreach

In the United Republic of Tanzania, a National Micro Finance Policy (2001) was formulated in recognition of the problem of access to financial services. The policy emphasizes the need for financial services to MSEs through the Bank of the United Republic of Tanzania, commercial banks and Savings, Credit and Cooperative Societies, all of which have been encouraged to introduce new programmes. Special funds have also been established for women and young people, mainly using existing institutions. The National Micro Finance Bank was also set up recently in the United Republic of Tanzania to take a lead role in this field, with some 95 branches planned.

Among the countries under study, Chile had the most successful policies to facilitate MSEs' access to financial markets (box 4.9), but there were few successful examples in the other countries. Some countries have policies and laws designed to promote national development, savings and investment. For example, Viet Nam has a Law on Encouraging Domestic Investment. However, these policies and laws rarely benefit MSEs.

Few countries have designed and implemented policies to improve access of MSEs to the banking system

Micro-credit services for MSEs in South Africa have been encouraged by providing exemptions to the Usury Act (1968)

Box 4.9   Finance policies for MSEs in Chile

Since the mid-1990s, Chile has been quite successful in incorporating MSEs into the banking system. In 1997, 44 per cent of all micro-enterprises and 66 per cent of all small enterprises registered with the tax authority, Servicio de Impuestos Internos, were indebted with the financial system. This credit coverage is higher than in other Latin American countries, such as Peru, Argentina and Mexico, and comes close to the coverage for developed countries (Inter-American Development Bank, 2002; Inversiones y Gestión Ltda., 2002). This success was due to a series of well-designed public policies, including the following:

- the existence of a well-functioning credit line for micro-enterprises managed by the Banco Estado, the main public finance institution of the country;
- the existence of credit lines for MSEs tendered by the State and administered by commercial banks; and
- the advanced development of financial regulations and the banking system, which has encouraged most private banks to reach out to MSEs as customers.

Despite these achievements, the economic slowdown that started in 1998 put many MSEs into a complicated financial situation which still affected the capacity of these enterprises to create employment four years later. In fact, while large enterprises managed to create new employment during the year following the brief recession in 1999, the MSE sector could not fully recover its previous level of employment.

The increase of interest rates during the adjustment period, as well as the change in the banks' attitude to a more conservative approach towards debtors perceived as risky, worsened the situation for many MSEs. Thus, MSEs remained heavily indebted with credit that was usually at high interest rates and short terms.

In order to help MSEs improve their financial situation and recover their employment creation potential, the Chilean Government announced a financial plan for SMEs in 2001. This plan included a programme to reschedule debts, involving a partial credit guarantee by the State.

This policy has been successful as far as the operation of the system is concerned, but the coverage is estimated to be insufficient compared to the real needs of Chile's MSEs. According to the MSE survey, 37 per cent of the enterprises with expired debt had used this policy, while 11 per cent were not even aware of the programme. Among the MSEs with current debt, 13 per cent had used the programme, while 18 per cent did not know about it (Espinosa 2001).

for small loans of less than 10,000 Rand (approximately US$800). This move was taken to "encourage the positive potential of the fast-growing micro loans sector and to limit the increasing abuses which have resulted in borrower over-indebtedness and the lack of credit access for small business" (Department of Trade and Industry, 2000, p. 63). However, while this policy shift has had a significant impact on the growth of micro-lenders in the finance sector, there is little evidence as yet to show that it has had a positive impact on the access of MSEs to finance.

In some countries, there are clear biases against women in finance policies. These biases affect micro-enterprises more than larger enterprises because women are relatively more prominent in this sector. Furthermore, while women tend to have easier access to micro-credit, when it comes to developing and expanding their micro-enterprises, they experience difficulties in accessing the necessary credit, and on appropriate terms, to enable them to finance business expansion. In South Africa, for example, women who were married in traditional or customary marriages used to have very limited capacity to enter into contracts with financial institutions. Through the enactment of the Customary Marriages Act (1998) women can now run their businesses more easily, as long as they have registered their marriages (Ntsika, 1999).

Finance policies can be biased against women

In Chile, Guinea, Peru and the United Republic of Tanzania, compliance with registration requirements in other policy fields, such as business registration, taxation and labour, helped MSEs obtain credit from formal credit providers. In Pakistan, South Africa and Viet Nam, a more mixed pattern can be observed for enterprises with partial compliance. However, in all seven countries, enterprises that do not comply with any of the basic registration requirements have less access to credit than those enterprises that complied with all of them (figure 4.4). Moreover, compliance also reduced the risk of applying for credit and being rejected by the financial institution.

Compliance with regulations helps MSEs to obtain credit

There are a number of explanations for this positive cor-relation between compliance with regulations and access to finance. First, in many countries, some kind of registration is simply necessary to identify the enterprise in order to grant it

Figure 4.4 Formal credit access by compliance with basic registration requirements, 2001 (percentages)

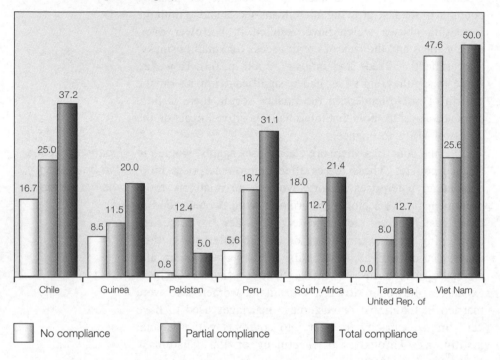

No compliance · Partial compliance · Total compliance

Note: Formal credit refers to business loans from a private or public bank, a Government credit fund or an international project. For more details on the registration requirements, see Chapter 3 and table A.4 in the Annex.

Source: ILO MSE Surveys, 2001.

credit. Second, in some contexts, the existence of effective health insurance and life insurance is a condition for obtaining a loan.[13] These insurance schemes diminish the risk of credit default due to accidents, illness or death of the MSE owner-manager. Third, compliance with regulations can often facilitate establishing a clear track record of the enterprise's past economic activity. Thus, policies that reduce the cost of compliance as lined out in Chapter 3 could improve MSEs' credit access.

---

[13] The synergies between insurance and credit can also work the other way around: micro-finance institutions can play an important role in extending the accessibility of life insurance products to low-income households and micro-enterprises (Churchill et al., 2002). However, a case study on South Africa suggests that this potential has not been fully explored yet (Aliber, 2002).

4.2 Findings on the combined impact of the policy fields

The policies and laws reviewed above display a consistent bias against MSEs either in their design or implementation stages, or both. Such biases undermine the potential of MSEs to contribute fully to the national promotion of decent work as well as the attainment of many other economic and social development goals. Policies, laws and regulations should provide a level playing field for enterprises of all size classes to grow and to create employment. While large modern enterprises often appear as more attractive targets of government support, they are also more capital-intensive than smaller enterprises. Biases in favour of large enterprises may therefore negatively affect the employment performance of an economy and increase poverty. To this point, this chapter has provided an account of the assessment of six policy fields drawing from the research in the selected countries. This has highlighted a number of common characteristics and functions of these policy fields, which can be used to identify those factors that influence employment in the MSE sector.

It is often difficult to assess whether the policy environment of a given country is biased against MSEs or not. In most cases, some policies favour small enterprises, while others favour large enterprises. For example, in Thailand, small manufacturing enterprises receive the majority of direct government subsidies. However, the full amount of these subsidies is very small and averages less than 0.1 per cent of all receipts of small enterprises. On the other hand, investment incentives from the Thai Board of Investment, which include exemptions from import duties on machinery and exemptions from corporate income tax for new projects, clearly favour larger enterprises. Almost one-third of the enterprises with more than 200 workers receive these benefits, while the share is only 2 per cent for small enterprises and even less for micro-enterprises.[14]

Despite good policy intentions, the environment in many countries is still biased against MSEs

Policy measures that appear to be neutral to enterprise size can also turn out to be biased against MSEs. During the economic

---

[14] Data refer to manufacturing establishments (single units) and include all forms of legal organization. Source: National Statistical Office of Thailand based on data from the Industrial Census, 1996.

adjustment in Chile in 1998, for example, the Central Bank increased interest rates dramatically. Commercial banks passed these increases on to their clients, and MSEs that have a higher share of short-term loans than larger enterprises were affected most. In addition, unlike many large enterprises, MSEs do not have access to international capital markets.

Many countries have support programmes for small enterprises while the overall economic policies are biased in favour of large enterprises. Specific support programmes may compensate the bias in the overall policies, but there is a risk that many enterprises suffer from the anti-small bias without being able to benefit from the specific programmes in favour of small enterprises. Another risk of policies that are specifically oriented towards helping the smallest enterprises is that by creating conditions that are more favourable for this size class they may convert themselves into growth-constraining policies for enterprises that are close in size to the maximum threshold of these benefits.

MSEs face lower labour costs but higher capital costs than larger enterprises

While MSEs often have lower operational costs through exemptions or evasion in the fields of labour and tax policies, MSEs face much higher costs in their access to credit. Haggblade et al. (1990) assess the policy bias in the 1960s and 1970s by analysing policy-induced price differentials. Compared to large enterprises, small enterprises in general face lower labour costs but higher capital costs than their larger counterparts. The difference in labour costs is generally less important than that in capital costs, resulting in a negative bias against small enterprises when these two fields are considered together. Trade policies are also often biased against MSEs. An analysis of more recent data from the 1990s, carried out as part of this research, confirms that despite the policy reforms during the last decades, the combined policy bias against MSEs in many developing countries continues to exist (Xtenina, 2000).[15]

There are common problems in policy design

The design of policies and laws that are responsive to the circumstances of MSEs and contribute to an environment that is conducive to more and better employment in the MSE sector appears to be influenced by three fundamental problems.

First, policies and laws are often designed without an adequate understanding of the MSE sector. Government

---

[15] Unfortunately, there are no estimates of the net employment effects of factor price changes (Haggblade et al., 1990), which makes it impossible to assess the precise overall employment impact of these biases.

officials and policy-makers appear to have inadequate information about the dynamics and circumstances that affect performance in MSEs. Thus, better information on the needs, opportunities and dynamics of the MSE sector is required.

Second, MSEs are not well represented in policy-making processes, and are often poorly organized as a sector. As a consequence, their representation and advocacy channels are weak, especially when compared to those of larger enterprises. Many chambers of commerce and even small business associations are dominated by medium-sized and large enterprises, and tend to present the case for enterprises of these size classes over those of the small enterprise. MSEs hold little political "clout" when it comes to policy reform and the intro-duction of policies that may be more enabling of the sector. Medium and large enterprises can be expected to lobby for the maintenance of the status quo in which they benefit from the bias in policy design.

The third fundamental problem in policy design that was uncovered in this research was the general lack of understanding among policy-makers regarding the ways government can enable, manage and monitor the MSE sector. The policies reviewed in this research were overwhelmingly dominated by regulatory and restrictive functions. Governments in all seven countries appeared to view the enterprise sector with suspicion and sought to control it wherever this was possible. While the regulatory and restrictive functions of government policy are readily accepted, this emphasis of policy is unbalanced.

For better or for worse, institutions and other mechanisms of implementation strongly influence the impact of policies and laws on employment in MSEs. This can mean that the original intentions of policy-makers are not visible in the final effects on MSEs. One of the most common problems that these mediating institutions face is the lack of a clear imple-mentation strategy in which all parties, both governmental and non-governmental, understand their responsibilities. The lack of coordination among government ministries and other development agents is also a major problem, as are those situations where there are poor or inadequate institutional arrangements for implementation.

There is a significant gap between the design of national policies regarding MSEs and their effective implementation

The role of the State in small enterprise development is influenced by the way the State is organized and the institutional framework it is built upon. There are competing social and economic agendas that the State decides upon which can fragment its response to the MSE sector. Effective implementation requires a combination of technical, strategic and political capacities. Often economic and social conditions change with such speed that the State is left in perpetual catch-up mode, where the policy design and implementation cycle is years behind. Moreover, the relationship between the public and the private sectors is not always a cooperative one. Governments can face resistance to changes in the political and legal environment, whether this is in the form of non-compliance by MSEs, or by outright opposition and advocacy by large enterprises.

Thus, the reality does not correspond to the formulated policies and the intentions of policy-makers

These implementation deficits can occur despite a high incidence of inspections among MSEs. In the United Republic of Tanzania, for example, MSEs reported a high incidence of government inspections and yet suffer from major problems in policy implementation. As table 4.8 shows, small enterprises are visited more often than their micro counterparts. This can be explained by the lower rates of registrations of micro-enterprises, as well as by the fact that micro-enterprises tend to be less visible than small enterprises. Moreover, in some countries, governments pay less attention to micro-enterprises.

In Pakistan and the United Republic of Tanzania, the survey question concerning government inspections was further adapted to distinguish between various government agencies. In both countries, the rates were higher for visits by tax officials than for visits by officials of any other government agency. In the United Republic of Tanzania, the rates for tax inspection were higher than the rates for tax registration, illustrating that some MSEs have to pay taxes even though they may not be registered with tax authorities.

Inspection visits can only be a useful tool for policy implementation when they are based on transparent and fair procedures. The combination of frequent inspections and low compliance found in several countries raises the question of whether other means of government action may also be effective in increasing compliance.

A first obvious field of action is to make information on regulatory requirements and entitlements available in the languages that MSE owner-managers can understand. To date, many regulations are drafted in the "wrong" language (this is

Table 4.8   Surveyed MSEs visited by government officials during last two years, 2001
(percentages)

	Micro	Small
Chile	55.3	64.7
Guinea	15.4	44.2
Pakistan	43.0	60.4
Peru	35.7	64.3
South Africa	23.7	60.0
Tanzania, United Rep. of	95.0	94.9
Viet Nam	28.6	40.7

Source: ILO MSE Surveys 2001.

the case in Guinea, Pakistan and the United Republic of Tanzania). Further consideration should be given to the facilitation role that government can perform in helping MSEs meet their legal and regulatory requirements.

Second, one-stop shops which allow easy registration and provide information on legal obligations as well as on available benefits can be another tool for better implementation. However, not all experiences with one-stop shops have been fully successful. In Guinea, the only one-stop shop is located in the capital, Conakry, which makes it less convenient for enterprises elsewhere in the country. In Peru, the lack of coordination between the Ministry of Industry and the tax authorities hampered the smooth operation of the one-stop shops.

A well-designed policy environment has low costs and high benefits for MSEs to incorporate themselves into the regulatory framework. It enables MSEs to move into new markets and creates synergies between public policies and market development. Indeed, market development and policies go hand in hand. The most important constraints for MSEs outside the regulatory framework are their limited access to markets. Complying with legal and regulatory requirements not only makes an enterprise "legal" in the eyes of government authorities; it also makes it more trustworthy in the eyes of potential business partners. As shown in Chapter 3, MSEs that comply with government regulations tend to perform better and create more employment than those enterprises that do not comply.

The paradox of positive MSE promotion in the context of a biased and stifling environment

In this chapter, we have identified common problems and examples in six policy fields that are particularly relevant for MSEs. We have also described some cross-cutting principles of policy design implementation to make the policy environment more conducive to MSEs' growth and employment creation. In Chapter 5, we present some guidance on how to initiate reforms of the policy environment.

IMPROVING THE POLICY AND LEGAL ENVIRONMENT

5

Changes to the policy and legal environment in which MSEs operate can have a significant effect on the performance and growth of MSEs, the volume and quality of employment they create, and the rate at which new enterprises are established. Regardless of the economic sector they operate within, their rural or urban location, or the sex of their owner-managers, enterprises are influenced by the policies and laws that surround them – whether they choose to comply with them or not. The challenge for governments is to create a policy and legal environment that is more enabling for the growth and improvement of employment in the MSE sector for all sectors, in all locations and for both sexes.

The previous chapters have shown how policies and laws can create an environment that is conducive to economic growth. They have also shown how specific policies, laws and regulations can undermine the potential of MSEs to operate effectively and to create more and better jobs for women and men. Policies and laws can create unnecessary and unproductive burdens on the MSE sector, whether from faults in their design or implementation. Governments can also overlook opportunities to use policy incentives to encourage enterprise registration and compliance, and to facilitate access to new markets.

Drawing from the research findings presented in the previous chapters, we formulate some general principles for reforming the policy, legal and regulatory environment. Focusing once more on the six policy fields, we make recommendations on the roles that various stakeholders can play in the processes of this reform.

5.1 General principles of reform

As we have seen, policies and laws rarely affect enterprise behaviour in a direct or singular way. Their influence on MSEs is determined by both their design and the mechanisms of implementation. Some policies and laws can alter the effect of other policies and laws. This effect can be cumulative, competitive and contradictory. Thus, reforming the policy and legal environment in which MSEs operate requires a comprehensive and systematic assessment of their impact on the MSE sector.

The findings presented in this book can help reform the policy and legal environment

The previous chapter presented the assessment of six policy fields and identified some common problems and basic principles for policy design and implementation. The findings presented in this book can be used to help reform the policy and legal environment in various countries so that the job creation potential of MSEs is enhanced, and the quality of employment in this sector is improved. We present first the cross-cutting principles for MSE policy reform before going into the six policy fields described in Chapter 4.

While many details of the design and implementation of the policy environment are specific to policy fields, some basic principles emerge

There is no blueprint or easy recipe for designing a policy environment that is conducive to more and better jobs in MSEs. However, there are a number of approaches to identifying reform targets that inform both the content of reforms and the processes such reforms should follow. Our research has highlighted seven general principles for improving the policy and legal environment.

1. Policies and laws need to be country specific. They should respond to the economic, social, legal and cultural context of each country, including the national distribution of small enterprises. They should also be tailored to the administrative systems of government. A law that works extremely well in one legal context may not work in another, simply because the situation and the legal system are different. For example, a reform of labour law would be different in Pakistan, where micro-enterprises have so far been exempted from most laws, than in Peru, where the majority of labour laws do in principle apply to all enterprises with paid workers.

2. Policies and laws should provide a level playing field for enterprises of all size classes. While it is not always easy to analyse whether a specific policy or set of policies favours smaller or larger enterprises, analytical tools can help to screen existing policies and regulations and their implementation. For example, an analysis of trade policies may reveal that economic sectors where large enterprises are dominant receive higher rates of effective protection than MSE-dominated sectors. In general, MSEs are most affected by transaction costs that are proportionally higher for them than for medium-sized or large enterprises and therefore they will benefit from reforms that lower these costs.

3. Sound and effective policies and laws require legitimacy. Solutions that are "parachuted" into a country without having been properly discussed by national stakeholders lack legitimacy. This is an issue of both democratic process and efficiency. Thus, the design of policy and law should involve all relevant stakeholders because failure in legitimacy will probably lead to a failure in implementation. Resistance from one or more of the main stakeholders can even block implementation completely. Effective implementation requires coordination across various government agencies, for example, to avoid duplication and to facilitate MSEs' dealings with government. Lack of coordination will hinder effective implementation. Laws that appear to be "good practice" on paper do not help anyone if they are not implemented.

4. Policies and laws must take account of existing gender-based inequalities – be they enshrined in current legislation, or embedded in the dominant culture and traditions – and ensure equality of treatment, access and control for women and men alike, both in the formulation process and in implementation. Many policies affecting MSEs do not consider or respond to the fact that their impact will not be the same for both sexes. Sometimes, gender biases cannot be eliminated by reforming laws in isolation from other policies. For example, in some countries the key to improving women's access to formal credit lies not within the field of finance policies, but in establishing equal property rights for men and women so that women can use their assets as collateral.

5. Transparency and communication are important elements of improving the policy environment. MSE owner-managers should be able to easily understand the policies and laws that affect their enterprises. Policies, laws and regulations should be clearly written in the most common languages used in the country. For example, in Pakistan, staff in large enterprises may be at ease in reading and understanding English, but guidelines in Urdu are necessary for the majority of MSE owner-managers. In some cases, especially where literacy is low, other forms of media should be used, such as radio and television. Policies and laws should also be implemented in a transparent way. The more understandable laws and regulations are, the less vulnerable MSEs are to arbitrary administrative decisions and corrupt practices. Where appropriate, mechanisms for the tracking of administrative procedures and appeal processes should be established so as to ensure transparency and fairness.

6. The design of policies and laws should be accompanied by a commitment to successful implementation. Policies and laws are easily rendered meaningless by lack of an implementation plan, by weak institutions or by poor coordination between the bodies responsible for implementation. Thus, successful implementation requires attention to the coordination of government and non-governmental services, in order to prevent overlaps and contradictions between different laws, regulations and the agencies that process and apply them. Simplification and harmonization across government agencies not only reduce the cost of compliance, but also maximize the benefits of compliance and save valuable public resources. Successful implementation can often require improvements in the systems of governance. The enforcement of laws and regulations, and the administration of promotional policies and programmes require transparent and practical procedures. Government should ensure that there are mechanisms for monitoring progress and for public accountability.

7. The last general principle for improving the policy and legal environment is concerned with the impact that policies and laws have on the MSE sector. Governments and other stakeholders should improve their information base on the

policy environment and its impact on MSEs. Policies and laws should be regularly assessed to determine the impact they have on MSE behaviour. In some countries, new economic legislation cannot be passed unless a favourable impact assessment has been made to determine the likely consequences it will have for MSEs. Among the seven countries under study, we presented the case of South Africa, where a study on the likely impact of new labour legislation on MSEs was carried out before deciding the details of implementation. The information base upon which policy-makers and legislators act should also include up-to-date statistical data on the contribution of MSEs to employment and GDP, as well as on the job quality in these enterprises.

These seven principles provide a foundation for good policy-making and implementation. They provide a framework for the process of policy design, implementation and assessment, and while they remain general in nature, they can contribute to the creation of a policy and legal environment that is more conducive to more and better jobs in MSEs. From this position we turn to a series of more specific recommendations.

5.2 Reform agendas within the six policy fields

In addition to the seven general principles for reform described above, our study has helped us unveil a number of useful approaches to identify reform targets that are specific to the six policy fields analysed in Chapter 4.

5.2.1 Reforms through the introduction of specific small enterprise promotion policies

Small enterprise promotion policies can provide a useful framework for reform. However, they usually do not provide solutions on their own. Granting benefits to MSEs has not been found to compensate for anti-MSE biases in the overall economic policies of a country. Nevertheless, when properly formulated and implemented, these policies can serve as a tool to start a process of improving the policy and legal environment

Small enterprise promotion policies can be a useful tool for policy reform

and establishing mechanisms to provide services to these enterprises. They can:

- establish a national definition for private micro-, small, medium and large enterprises, which is used by all government ministries and development agents;
- prescribe a process of assessment and review for the introduction of any new economic policies and laws that may affect the enterprise sector (through the requirement for a small enterprise impact assessment report, for example);
- enhance the coordination of efforts (policies, programmes, services) across all government ministries;
- articulate government's vision for the enterprise sector – particularly in terms of job creation and other ways of achieving national social and economic goals;
- ascribe specific rights and responsibilities to the enterprise sector (such as the protection of business names, limited liability for incorporated entities, public reporting obligations, anti-monopoly protection);
- establish incentives for enterprises to innovate and to increase their productivity (for example, through partial subsidies on expenses for research and development and hiring consultants);
- create an institutional framework in which enterprises can be represented and supported;
- identify and eliminate inequalities or barriers (be they planned or accidental) that disadvantage people based on sex, ethnicity, disability, and so forth; and
- identify indicators and mechanisms for assessing the performance of the enterprise sector and ways in which the policy, legal or institutional framework can be improved.

While we have found problems with some of the small enterprise policies assessed in this study – in terms of both design and implementation – such policy instruments can provide a much-needed focus on the MSE sector. Thus, they have enormous potential as a tool for reform.

5.2.2   Reforming business laws and regulations

Business laws and regulations are often complex, confusing and costly. While all enterprises are affected by the loss of time and money to comply with these regulations, the burden is heavier for MSEs than for larger enterprises.

The design of business laws and regulations can be improved by simplifying them as far as possible and by eliminating those regulations that do not serve any purpose. In particular, overlaps and contradictions between registration requirements with different agencies should be eliminated. Reporting requirements, such as reporting frequencies and format, can be harmonized across government agencies, and licences may, in some cases, be replaced with simple registration requirements with reduced discretionary power for government officials. Box 5.1 summarizes the efforts to improve the design and implementation of business laws and regulations in six of the countries under study.[1]

Many business laws and regulations can be simplified

A number of other countries have simplified their procedures relating to the regulation of business practices. In general, the aim of these reforms is to lower the costs of compliance – either directly or indirectly. These reforms affect either the design or the implementation of laws and regulations. For example, Kenya has started to reform its system of business licences from a system requiring enterprises to hold multiple business licences for each activity to a simplified system where each enterprise requires only a Single Business Permit (SBP). The time and travel costs for the licensing process for small enterprises fell by 23 per cent between 1997 and 1999 in the localities where the SBP had been adopted, while they increased by 9 per cent in the non-SBP localities (Abuodha and Bowles, 2000a). A similar approach to reform could be used in many other countries where complex systems of multiple licences prevail.

On the implementation side, one-stop shops can be used to facilitate registration, allowing potential and existing enterprises to obtain all necessary information and to initiate registration procedures in one single administrative entity (OECD, 1999). This saves both governments' and enterprises' resources. The government could re-invest these savings by improving the regional and provincial coverage of one-stop shops for registration. However, some of these initiatives turn out to be less

---

[1] Legislative reforms in Pakistan are still at the proposal stage. Moreover, they are focused on tax and labour law rather than on business regulation, as these are the more urgent areas for change in Pakistan.

Box 5.1	Reforms of business laws and regulations, and their effects
Chile	The procedures to obtain a municipal permit have been improved in many municipalities, reducing the time and the number of documents required. Further simplification of regulations has started for family-based micro-enterprises.
Guinea	A one-stop shop was initiated by the Office de Promotion des Investissements Privés, established in 1992. However, this one-stop shop was only available in the capital city, which strongly reduced its value for enterprises in smaller towns or in rural areas.
Peru	Business laws and regulations have been simplified during the 1980s and 1990s. In 1984, it took 289 days to register a small manufacturing enterprise and the cost was US$1,231. By 1998, this time span had been reduced to 30 days and the cost involved had fallen to US$200. Enterprises in the trade sector have experienced similar improvements.
	A one-stop centre initiative failed due to the lack of coordination between the different agencies involved.
South Africa	The Department of Trade and Industry has begun to look more closely at the regulatory framework in which MSEs operate. While there has been growing criticism of the Government concerning the increasing number of laws and regulations introduced to govern small enterprises, the Department has recently commissioned research into the cost of compliance to determine the effect this has on small enterprises.
Tanzania, United Republic of	There are ongoing efforts to simplify the procedures related to the registration and licensing of enterprises. For example, it has been decided to transfer the registration and licensing of micro- and small enterprises to district councils.
	One-stop shops have been introduced for foreign investors, but not for domestic enterprises, creating a bias against MSEs.
Viet Nam	The Enterprise Law, introduced in 2000, replaced case-by-case discretionary approval of new enterprises with streamlined registration procedures. It reduced the number of steps required to register an enterprise from 13 to seven, the average time needed to register a business decreased from 99 days to 17 days and the average monetary cost involved dropped from US$660 to about US$30.

Source: Country papers.

useful than planned due to a lack of coordination or because the initiative is limited to the capital city (see box 5.1).

There are a number of approaches to lower the compliance costs for MSEs and enterprises in general. These include:

- reducing fees and other costs, including initial registration costs and the ongoing payments required to remain formal;
- streamlining regulatory procedures, sometimes by centralizing and improving the coordination of multiple government agencies (for example, establishing one-stop shops);
- setting up government agencies for registration and information close to where MSEs are, so as to avoid expensive and time-consuming travel;
- using the Internet where appropriate to carry out administrative interactions online;
- introducing self-reporting schemes where appropriate to reduce the number of inspection visits; and
- contracting business associations for procedures and service delivery where this is more cost-effective.

Finally, in addition to making compliance with laws and regulations easier, policy-makers and legislators need to ensure that compliance also brings tangible benefits for MSEs. Enterprise owner-managers need to be shown how compliance is not only an official obligation but also good practice, which is accompanied by relevant rights, protections and rewards.

5.2.3 Improving labour policies, laws and regulations for the MSE sector

The challenge to improving the policies, laws and regulations surrounding labour in MSEs is to find ways to ensure the basic rights of workers in MSEs which are consistent with the situation and resource constraints of these enterprises. In many cases, the prevailing labour laws and regulations affecting MSEs are old and outdated. Thus, reform in this policy field requires a reappraisal of the labour issues facing MSEs and their workers so that labour laws and regulations can be modernized. Once this is done, new mechanisms for implementation can be introduced. Box 5.2 describes the example of Chile, where a new strategy of legal enforcement among micro-enterprises has been established

Box 5.2   Enforcing labour law in Chilean micro-enterprises: Replacing fines with training

Enforcing labour laws in micro-enterprises is often difficult because entrepreneurs are not always aware of their legal obligations.

Since the latest labour law reform in Chile in 2001, micro-enterprises with nine or fewer employees found guilty of violating the labour law can replace their fine upon request with a compulsory training programme. These courses last a maximum of two weeks and are organized by the labour administration (Dirección del Trabajo). If the employer does not attend the training course within two months, the original fine is doubled. The conversion of fines into training is limited to one breach of labour law per year.

This new initiative is part of a series of efforts by the Chilean Government to connect labour inspections to the broader activities of promoting sound industrial relations and an appropriate understanding of labour law by all employers in the country.

Source: ILO/SEED based on the Código del Trabajo, Article 477.

which permits employers to opt for a compulsory training course on labour law instead of paying a fine.

Simplifying procedures and reducing the number of laws and regulations MSE owner-managers are bound by can facilitate compliance with labour laws. However, our study has highlighted the dangers that arise when exempting MSEs from their obligations under labour law. This not only leaves workers unprotected, it creates growth traps for enterprises close to the maximum threshold for the exemption.[2] Partial exemptions for MSEs should only be based on careful analysis of the impact of the law or regulation under consideration.

Social dialogue is an important means of implementing labour regulations. However, the participation of MSEs in social dialogue is often insufficient, as illustrated be the low rates of unionization and affiliation to employers' organizations, chambers of commerce and small enterprise associations. Beyond their duty to protect the right of workers and employers to organize, governments should recognize the role of stakeholders as interlocutors and partners in policy-making and programme implementation at national and local levels (ILO, 2002b).

---

[2] In addition to the negative consequences for employment creation and employment quality, such exemption may also undermine the incentives for MSEs to upgrade their production and to produce for more demanding markets (Tendler, 2002).

The coverage of social security among MSE owners and workers is low in most of the seven countries under study. This has a direct impact on the quality of life of these persons, and can often lead into poverty in cases of accident, illness or disability. Extending the social security system to MSEs therefore is a key policy challenge.

Health care is a priority because it is an urgent need where the benefits from improved coverage are clearly visible. Such programmes can provide general or work-related medical and hospital treatment for sickness and accidents. A second priority would be a programme of cash benefits for old age, disability and death. Moreover, the measures to extend the coverage for MSE owners and workers should be complementary to any tax-based social benefits, so that the poverty-reduction potential is fully explored (Ginneken, 2003). Finally, special emphasis should be placed on measures to ensure that women are fully included in social protection schemes.

Governments have a key role to facilitate the extension of mechanisms for social security and social dialogue to MSEs

There are different ways to include MSEs into the coverage of social security (ILO, 2000b):

- Adapt existing social security schemes to facilitate the extension of coverage to employees in MSEs and to the self-employed (see box 5.3 for the examples of Thailand and the Republic of Korea). This has to be done gradually and in parallel with the strengthening of administrative capacities.

- Establish special schemes for certain categories of workers in MSEs, taking into account their often-reduced capacity to contribute.

- Restructure the administration to facilitate registration and the collection of contributions, to improve customer service and to strengthen compliance.

- Promote micro-insurance schemes that have the advantages of cohesion, direct participation and low administrative costs. Health insurance schemes for MSE workers can either cover high-cost, low-frequency events (for example, hospital care), or low-cost, high-frequency events (such as primary health care). Governments can support and promote the development of micro-insurance by improving the availability of quality health services for all and by creating an appropriate legal and fiscal framework.

Box 5.3   Extending social security to MSEs: Examples from the Republic of Korea
             and Thailand

A number of countries have made efforts to extend and improve social security coverage
by gradually bringing smaller enterprises into the system.

The Republic of Korea has increased the coverage of health insurance dramatically over
a relatively short time span. In 1977, the first group to be covered by compulsory health
insurance were employees of large enterprises with more than 500 workers. Over the
following years progressively smaller enterprises were included. In 1988, coverage was
extended to enterprises with more than five employees. Coverage was extended even
further to the self-employed, using a government subsidy to alleviate the burden of
contributions for this category.

In Thailand, a social security scheme for private sector workers was introduced in 1990.
The scheme started with health insurance for workers in enterprises with 20 or more
employees. It was then gradually extended, both in its benefits and in its coverage. The
scheme currently includes insurance in case of sickness, maternity, invalidity and death,
as well as a pension scheme. As from September 1993, workers in enterprises with ten
or more workers were included in the coverage and in April 2002, the social security
coverage was extended to non-agricultural enterprises with at least one employee.
During the first 12 months after the inclusion of enterprises with fewer than ten
employees, the number of registered establishments jumped up from 116,000 to
308,000, while the number of insured workers increased from 6.0 million to 7.1 million.
Although this increase is substantial, it is estimated that at least one million more workers
are legally entitled to social security coverage.

Sources: ILO/SEED based on Kwon (2002), Schramm (2002) and data from the Social Security Office of Thailand
(http://www.sso.molsw.go.th).

5.2.4   Reforming taxation policies, laws and regulations

Taxation must be
fair to MSEs and
result in improved
delivery of public
services

Because they are productive units, private enterprises,
regardless of their size, are often able to provide funds to
state revenue – indeed, in many countries the revenue-raising
potential of enterprises has been emphasized. While some
countries have already succeeded in simplifying their
taxation systems (box 5.4 describes the example of Peru), in
most countries, taxation is still too complex for MSEs.
Moreover, in some countries, taxation rates are too high
for MSEs.

Box 5.4   Simplifying taxation in Peru: Success and remaining challenges

Until the late 1980s, Peru was characterized by a complex tax system with various levels of tax rates and exemption schemes for different types of economic units. During the early 1990s, the Peruvian authorities started a major reform of the tax system in order to make it more efficient. The main principles of reform were the simplification of the tax system, the concentration of tax administration in one single tax authority, the Superintendencia National de Administración Tributaria (SUNAT), and the introduction of simple procedures for compliance. The reform also abolished a number of requirements for tax registration that were not considered necessary, and eliminated 62 taxes.

In order to facilitate the entry of micro-enterprises into the system, two special tax regimes were established: the Régimen Especial del Impuesto a la Renta (RER) for enterprises with yearly revenues below US$60,000, and the Régimen Unico Simplificado (RUS), limited to unincorporated enterprises selling to final consumers. These two tax regimes with low costs of compliance succeeded in broadening the net of taxpayers considerably. In 1999, there were 134,000 registered taxpayers under the RER and 595,000 under the RUS.

Despite these achievements and the recognized efficiency of the SUNAT, the Peruvian taxation system for MSEs also has its problems. For example, the State spends 75 cents in remunerations for each dollar of tax revenue obtained through the RUS. This is five times more than for each dollar of tax revenue under the RER and 119 times more than under the general tax regime.

Sources: Chacaltana (2001) and Tokman et al. (2001).

The review of taxation policies, laws and regulations includes different types of taxes, such as income taxes, profit taxes, VAT, capital taxes and tax incentive schemes. The main steps for the reform of tax systems include the following (Tokman et al., 2001):

• Eliminate anti-MSE biases caused by flat-rate taxes and duplicated taxation of economic activities at various stages.
• Reduce the costs of compliance by simplifying the procedures for compliance and the tax forms and by minimizing administrative costs for taxpayers. This can be done both by reducing the number of taxes to be paid and by eliminating unnecessary requirements for compliance. Administrative fees for tax registration should be avoided as they can create incentives for remaining informal.

- Create an appropriate single infrastructure for tax collection. This helps to avoid the duplication of responsibilities and thus lowers the costs of tax collection both for the State and for MSEs, who can then interact with one single tax authority. A single tax agency also facilitates effective enforcement.
- Improve the delivery of services financed from tax revenues and demonstrate the link between taxes and services by informing taxpayers.

5.2.5 Enhancing trade opportunities for MSEs through policy reform

Markets have been found in this study to influence the employment decisions of MSE owner-managers more than any other factor. Employment growth in the MSE sector and improvements in job quality are connected to the market opportunities that owner-managers perceive. Governments should facilitate and enhance the access MSEs have to markets, creating for them opportunities to broaden their market base and deepen market penetration, and intervening to correct market failures and dominant gender-based inequalities. This involves a range of policy portfolios, but one of the most relevant is trade.

Export incentives should be designed in an MSE-friendly manner   Although trade liberalization has reduced the bias against MSEs that was inherent in most import-substitution strategies, there are still many policy obstacles that keep MSEs from benefiting from international trade. The pattern and sequence in the reduction of import protection may also affect MSEs and larger enterprises differently. To give MSEs the same opportunities to benefit from international trade as larger enterprises it is important that export incentives schemes are designed and implemented in a way that MSEs can benefit. There are different measures to ensure that trade policies do not discriminate against MSEs:

- In the design of export incentive schemes, minimum export amounts should be avoided. Eligibility should not involve separate licensing or registration processes that cost time and money on top of the normal business registration.

- Import procedures should be simplified so that MSEs can easily import their inputs without depending on larger enterprises importing for them.
- MSEs' or MSE associations' participation in trade fairs can be supported so that producers are able to make their products known to potential clients.
- The reform of import tariffs should be monitored to ensure that the rates of effective protection do not discriminate against sectors dominated by MSEs compared to larger enterprises, as has often been the case in the past.

The measures described above concern international trade, but policy biases against MSEs also arise due to discrimination in domestic markets. For example, public tenders are often designed and implemented in a manner that makes it very difficult or even impossible for MSEs to participate. Government policies can play a crucial role in opening up public sector markets through the re-design of tendering procedures, including for labour-intensive infrastructure projects.

Creating new trade opportunities for MSEs not only involves creating special schemes or policies that open new markets specifically for MSEs, but requires a legal and regulatory framework that is more enabling and competitive. As discussed in Chapter 2, many MSEs suffer from adverse power relations and market exclusions. There are imbalances in the power relationships among enterprises of different size classes that exclude smaller enterprises from full and equal participation in the market. This can result from biases in the legal and regulatory frameworks as well as from the exclusions or imbalances in prevailing social relations, such as traditional relations that are prejudiced against women as property owners, or bonded labour situations.

To address these problems, governments should take three kinds of initiatives. First, they should examine the market information that is available to small enterprises and find ways to address situations where this information is found to be inadequate, out of date or hard for MSEs to obtain. Governments should not necessarily do this themselves, since it may be better to facilitate the generation and distribution of market information through private sector (for example, industry associations) and even community-based organizations.

Second, governments should systematically identify and remove biases in the policy and legal framework, such as biases against MSEs and against women-owned enterprises. This is a constant process that should involve the active participation of key stakeholders.

Third, governments should ensure that MSEs are directly connected to macroeconomic development strategies. This requires MSEs to be specifically incorporated into trade policies and programmes, strategic industry development policies and any other relevant policy field upon which the national development goals are framed.

As with other policy fields, changes in trade policy should be preceded by an analysis of the likely impact on enterprises of different size classes. This is critical if the potential benefits of globalization are to be extended to the poor and marginalized groups of society.

5.2.6 Reforming financial sector policies, laws and regulations for MSEs

Policies can reduce transaction costs and improve MSEs' access to formal credits

Many MSEs experience difficulties accessing credit from formal sources. In the case of start-ups and micro-enterprises, this is often due to the insufficient or inappropriate assets that can be used as collateral by owner-managers. In the case of small enterprises, the key constraints are the high transaction costs for borrowers and lenders: the costs of assessing the business project, establishing the collateral and monitoring the loan performance.

There were many examples found in this study of attempts to use existing financial institutions and special loan facilities to address some of the problems MSEs face in this regard. While some of these schemes work well, many face problems with sustainability and marginalizing MSEs from the mainstream of economic activity.

To obtain access to formal credit on a large scale, MSEs need policy solutions rather than programme interventions. There are four policy domains that require attention.

First, governments need to establish an institutional, legal and regulatory environment that encourages a diversity of financial institutions, allows healthy competition within the banking system, and facilitates credit access for MSEs with sound business projects. This includes, for example, the following legal instruments and institutions:

- Reforming collateral law to reduce transaction costs and to facilitate the use of collateral substitutes, especially for micro-enterprises and for women entrepreneurs, can help improve MSEs' access to credit (Balkenhol and Schütte, 2001).
- Rating agencies and credit bureaus can play an important role in reducing the information asymmetry problem, even though they might be more practical for the upper end of the small enterprise market.
- User-friendly registries to document ownership status are important to certify assets that can be used as collateral.
- Bankruptcy laws and contract enforcement (for example, small claims courts) are part of the general business regulations, but have an important role to play in improving credit markets for MSEs.

Second, in order to avoid duplication and market distortions, government interventions into financial markets should be based on the analysis of credit availability for different types of MSEs. For example, small enterprises may have sufficient access to short-term credit, but face credit rationing for longer-term finance.

Third, rather than directly giving credit to MSEs, governments can act as a second-tier bank by contracting funds to banks which in turn will make previously defined credit lines available to MSEs. Any subsidy elements should only reduce the transaction costs for banks and MSEs to establish loan arrangements, rather than reduce interest rates.

Governments should not directly provide credit to MSEs

Finally, governments should be aware that policies that supposedly have uniform application and effect across enterprises of different sizes, such as fiscal policies and exchange rate policies, could be biased against MSEs. For example, MSEs tend to have shorter-term credits than larger enterprises. They are, therefore, affected disproportionately by interest rate variations stemming from macroeconomic policy decisions.

5.3 Processes for reform

Having the right answers to questions regarding the best design of the policy environment does not guarantee that policies will actually be designed and implemented effectively. Effective reform of the policy and legal environment requires a process in which all relevant stakeholders can participate. Such processes should promote communication (sharing information, experiences and perspectives), agreement on reform priorities and strategies, and ultimately, legitimacy of reform outcomes.

The identification of potential targets for policy reform involves a continuing series of actions including analysis, targeting, revision and evaluation (box 5.5 lists a number of related tools and resources linked to these). There are two essential ingredients that lead to success in policy reform: process and participation. In this final part of the chapter we examine the processes and partners of policy reform. This is done by describing some of the broader processes involved in the reform of policies and laws, and then by presenting proposals to key stakeholders concerning the roles they can perform in these processes.

5.3.1 Processes for policy reform

Policy reforms should be based on an assessment of the current policy and legal environment if they are to be effective in creating more and better employment in the MSE sector. This should include an assessment of policy implementation. All too often, new policies are designed without a proper assessment of the weaknesses and possible biases against small enterprises in the current environment. Likewise, many countries have very attractive policies on paper, but suffer from insufficient implementation. The results are unintended consequences, overlaps between old and new policies, or "paper tigers".

Reforms should take place in a systematic way This approach to reform typically involves four critical steps. In the first place, it is essential to assess the policy and legal environment and to identify the main constraints or obstacles to MSE development and employment creation. This assessment should incorporate MSE stakeholders in the process. Once this has been done, the priorities for reform can be defined.

The second step may involve a search for good practices to identify how other governments have dealt with these issues. Such practices may then be adapted to fit national circumstances.

Third, policy reform should involve dialogue with various stakeholders, including representatives of the MSE sector,

Box 5.5   Tools and resources to aid policy reform[3]

The research presented in this book leads to some criteria and examples of good and bad practice that can be used to assess and reform the policy environment. The ILO has also developed several practical tools that can be used in this process. These include:

Tools and guidelines

Manual for the mapping and assessment of the policy and regulatory environment for MSEs, February 2001. Available in English and French.

This manual is a guide for national consultants involved in assessments of the impact of the policy environment on employment in MSEs. It offers a step-by-step approach to the process, and also provides a glossary of relevant terms and key contact information. The tool has subsequently been adapted for use in the context of more recent small enterprise development initiatives, for example in India, the Islamic Republic of Iran, Nepal and Paraguay.

Survey kit: How to measure the influence of national policies, laws and regulations on employment in micro and small enterprises, July 2002. Available in English, French and Spanish.

This manual contains the information required to conduct a survey designed to assess the influence of national policies, laws and regulations on decisions taken by MSE owner-managers. In addition to important information on the rationale of the approach, the kit contains a generic questionnaire that can be modified to suit the conditions of the survey country. It also contains guidelines for designing a sampling frame, along with recommendations for the organization, management and quality control of the survey.

Assessment tool kit: Tools and processes for assessing the policy and regulatory framework for small enterprise development, October 2002. Available in English.

The tool kit is based on the above Manual and Survey kit, and provides guidance on how to conduct a rapid yet systematic assessment of the policy and regulatory environment.

Training programmes

MSE development: Tools and methods for formulating policies and strategies. Available in French and English.

This is a training programme to raise stakeholders' awareness about the importance of the policy and legal environment for MSEs. This training manual has been developed for a project in French-speaking West Africa.

Cont./

---

[3] All the resources listed are available free of charge from ILO/SEED (IFP-SED@ilo.org), with the exception of *Policies and strategies for SME development*, which is available from the ILO International Training Centre, Turin (sme@itcilo.it).

Cont./

Providing a conducive local climate for MSEs: How local and provincial authorities can facilitate growth and reduction of poverty by creating an enabling environment for small businesses. Currently available in Vietnamese.

Adapted from the training programme *MSE development* for use in Viet Nam, this programme is intended to create awareness and skills among local authority staff about the advantages – in terms of economic growth, social gains, job creation and poverty alleviation – of supporting the private MSE sector.

Policies and strategies for SME development: How to design programmes to improve the enabling environment for SMEs. Available in English.

This is a training programme delivered by the ILO's International Training Centre, Turin, which aims at improving policy-makers' skills to analyse, design and implement policies and strategies for the development of SMEs in consultation with relevant stakeholders.

Other support

Guide to ILO Recommendation No. 189. Available in English, French, Spanish, Arabic, Russian and Vietnamese.

This booklet explains the content of the Job Creation in Small and Medium-Sized Enterprises Recommendation, 1998 (No. 189). The aim is to make the contents of the Recommendation known among relevant stakeholders. A conducive business environment is among the key topics addressed in the Recommendation.

Small enterprise development: An introduction to the policy challenge, August 2003. Available in English, French, Spanish, Arabic, Russian and Vietnamese.

This 32-page booklet, which expands upon Recommendation No. 189, introduces the policy and regulatory environment as an important external influence on the capacity of small enterprises to create more and better jobs.

The ILO headquarters in Geneva and its field offices work with key national counterparts to promote reforms in the policy and legal environment for small business and the employment dimensions associated with this sector. This work uses the research findings described above, as well as other information gained through consultative processes, to identify reform requirements and to set in train a process for reform that will lead to changes in the policy and legal environment that are more conducive to job creation for women and men and the improvement of working conditions within small enterprises. The promotion of gender equality is an integral part of this approach.

labour, civil society and any other relevant groups, such as associations of women entrepreneurs. Based on the knowledge of key constraints and on good practice used elsewhere, new laws and regulations can be designed and implemented.

Finally, reform measures should be closely monitored and, where necessary, fine-tuned or changed to achieve their desired result.

In theory, most countries use some kind of participatory approach in MSE policy reform. However, the extent to which participatory mechanisms actually shape the policy-making process varies strongly across countries. Many participatory processes work without quantifiable objectives or a specific time frame for designing and implementing reforms. Moreover, some roundtables or committees set up for reform spend most of their time discussing procedure and administrative matters. This often makes it difficult to carry forward and monitor the implementation of new policies (English and Hénault, 1995; Franz and Oesterdiekhoff, 1998; R. Gross, 2000).

Regardless of the formal set-up of the policy reform process, there can also be important differences between a "stakeholder-driven approach" and a "consultant-driven approach". The latter may lead to technically good policy recommendations, but decision-making and implementation are often hampered by a lack of ownership among the stakeholders. Similarly, while international agencies can facilitate reform processes, they should not sit in the driver's seat. When international experts prepare proposals for reforms without the active participation of local stakeholders, there is a strong risk that local ownership will be insufficient and follow-up on recommendations will not occur.[4]

On the other hand, task forces consisting only of representatives of local institutions may suffer from a lack of technical skills and budget to sustain operations. The most promising approach appears to lie in the interaction of predominantly local experts with selected external experts to generate recommendations on which there is a wide local consensus (Onyango and Tomecko, 1995).

---

[4] For more information on the role that international agencies can play in reforming the policy and legal environment, see White and Chacaltana (2002).

5.3.2 The role of key stakeholders in policy reform

The findings presented in this book have focused on the role of government in setting an environment that is conducive to the creation of more and better jobs in the MSE sector. While government has the primary responsibility for the design of a policy and legal framework and the creation and maintenance of the institutions that enforce this framework, the role of improving and reforming this environment should not be left to government alone. A central finding of this research has been the insufficient representation of the MSE sector in policy-making processes.

The ILO has sustained a commitment to the shared involvement of employer and worker organizations in the design and review of policies and laws that shape employment. Governments are encouraged to work with representatives of the MSE sector in the design of policy and laws that influence the volume and quality of employment in this sector. International labour Recommendation No. 189 is but one example of the agreements reached between representatives of governments, employers and workers on the issue of small enterprise development.

One reason for the large-enterprise bias of the policy environment in many countries is that small enterprises are "seldom organized in such a way as to have much involvement or influence on public policy-making" (Berry, 1995, p. 1). Moreover, informal economy organizations often lack a defined interface with those with whom they need top-level dialogue. Without recognition by government authorities, they have no voice in policy debates (ILO, 2002b). Although there are now many examples of small enterprise associations working with government, it is still very difficult for small enterprises to voice their interests, especially when they operate in the same sectors as larger enterprises.

Increasing the role of MSE owners and workers in social dialogue is an important means to improving their social and economic situation within the workplace and in a larger national context. Effective MSE representative bodies can make the voice of this category of enterprises heard in policy-making arenas to ensure the impact of new laws and regulations on the MSE sector is taken into account. MSE associations can also help develop the market for business development services for MSEs.

Social dialogue can be an important tool to bring about a fair balance between the interests of MSE owners and workers, whatever the structure and size of the enterprise. An important objective for both employers' and workers' organizations is therefore to extend their outreach among the smallest enterprises and the informal economy. These workers and employers may wish to join existing trade unions and employers' organizations, or they may want to form their own. Employers' and workers' organizations play a critical role in either strategy: enabling existing representative organizations to extend membership and services to MSEs, and encouraging and supporting the creation and development of new member-based, democratically managed representative organizations, including bringing them into social dialogue processes (ILO, 2002a). Such a strategy will enable stakeholders to participate more fully in the design and implementation of policies and laws that address the creation of more and better jobs in the MSE sector.

At a conference held by the ILO in Bangkok for representatives of governments, employers' and workers' organizations,[5] the following roles of employers' organizations were agreed upon:

The role of employers' organizations

- Advocacy: Employers' organizations should take a strong position in political debates to make their points of view known. They should also publicize their concerns and points of view through mass media. For example, they can advocate in favour of measures to soften the adverse effects of globalization and trade liberalization.
- Research and information: As MSEs often lack the necessary information to run and expand their business, employers' organizations can help them by carrying out research on various topics (such as market access, management techniques, technological upgrading) and provide information on these and other relevant matters to MSEs.

---

[5] Asia and Pacific regional training workshop on developing a conducive environment for micro- and small enterprise development (14–15 May 2001), Bangkok, Thailand. This workshop was organized jointly by the ILO Regional Office for Asia and the Pacific and ILO/SEED. It included participants from seven countries: Cambodia, East Timor, Indonesia, Pakistan, the Philippines, Thailand and Viet Nam.

- Facilitating access to credit: Employers' organizations should take an active role in improving MSEs' access to credit. This can be achieved through credit unions or by participating in guarantee schemes.
- Labour relations: Conflictive industrial relations with emerging trade unions can be particularly problematic in the small enterprise sector and in some cases constrain their development. Initiatives aiming at harmonious labour relations are therefore particularly useful for small enterprises.
- Coordinating and cooperating with community organizations: Employers' organizations should coordinate and cooperate with existing community organizations to promote projects in favour of MSEs and provide them with protection.
- Implementation of policies: The problems of implementation of government policies were identified as a key concern. Employers' organizations should help overcome this problem by developing proposals on how the implementation process could be accelerated.

Sometimes, women entrepreneurs perceive existing employers' and business associations as male-dominated and inappropriate to their needs. Consequently, they form their own associations of women entrepreneurs. Such associations should also be enabled to participate effectively in policy-making arenas.

The role of workers' organizations Workers' organizations, on the other hand, when addressing the challenge of MSE employment and participating in reform processes, may pursue a number of objectives that can enhance their contribution to a policy and legal environment that is more conducive to decent work in the MSE sector. They can obtain more knowledge about employment in the MSE sector as well as of small enterprise dynamics, and this knowledge can be used to identify worker needs, as well as to design adequate policy and legal responses. They can also extend their services to workers (and employers) within the MSE sector. They can take steps to involve unorganized workers in small enterprises and they can develop tools and approaches to labour relations in small enterprises that owner-managers can adopt in collaboration with their workers.

5.4 Conclusions

At the outset of this research, three broad research questions were formulated. These were presented in Chapter 1 and have provided the framework on which much of this study has been conducted. In answering these questions we have come to better understand how policy environments within nations influence the generation and quality of employment within MSEs, even though further research is necessary to fully understand the link between the policy and legal environment and MSE employment (box 5.6).

Through this research we have ascertained that the contribution MSEs make to employment is significant, but that it is largely a result of policies which have generated a great many new survivalist enterprises and increased poor-quality employment in the sector. While the contribution of policy factors to this situation has been identified, it is clear that it has not been created intentionally. Rather, it has come about through governments focusing on large enterprises too much and assuming that macroeconomic changes will benefit enterprises of all sizes. Although employment in MSEs has grown dramatically because of macroeconomic policies, this sector has become the poor relation of larger enterprises because of the absence of policies that respond to its experiences.

A well-designed policy and legal environment for MSE employment comes from removing the anti-MSE bias that has been found in all seven countries studied. Small enterprises can be better connected to the macroeconomic and social development strategies of a country by being put on an equal footing with larger enterprises. In addition, MSEs can be encouraged to comply with the laws of the land through a twofold process that enhances the capacity and desirability of enterprises to comply, while reviewing (that is, simplifying and streamlining) regulatory procedures. At the heart of such measures is the requirement for government to see itself as a facilitator of MSE promotion and not solely as a regulator.

Significantly, policies and laws are not effective on their own. To work, they require clear strategies for implementation and institutions that are accountable, transparent and efficient.

Box 5.6   Some ideas for further research

Further research is needed on the link between the policy environment for MSEs and the volume and quality of employment. Too little is known about the employment creation by different categories of enterprises – by size, registration status, or characteristics of its owner. There are still unanswered questions concerning the casual relationships between macroeconomic dynamics and the rates of MSE births and deaths. MSEs sometimes appear as the main victims in the event of economic downturns, while other studies emphasize the resilience of MSEs to these kinds of fluctuations. While the specific answers may vary from country to country as well as by economic sector, size and other characteristics of the MSE, more research into this topic could clearly help to design and implement better employment policies for MSEs to cope with crisis situations and create employment. This requires the longitudinal analysis of employment flows based on establishment-level data.

In addition, the impact of different types of policy and regulatory environment has not been studied sufficiently. The measurement of the impact of different policies is still extremely difficult. While several tools have been developed to monitor the progress of policy reform, no comprehensive methodology exists to study the impact of these reforms. Quasi-experimental methods used to assess the impact of programme and project interventions can rarely be used due to the lack of a proper control group. The multitude of relevant factors is also difficult to disentangle by any analytical method. The only available approach for now consists of careful comparisons between the situation before and after reform, as well as across countries and regions.

Finally, while this research and other information gained from previous studies have allowed us to define some principles for the design and implementation of appropriate labour policies for MSEs, further research on this topic is necessary. Standard economic analysis often provides a one-sided view of labour regulations, which focuses exclusively on the costs of such regulations. However, in order to meet the twin challenge of protecting workers and enhancing employment creation, it is crucial to analyse the benefits of labour laws and the resulting actual impact on both enterprises and workers. This is clearly a priority topic for the ILO.

Governments have to consider their broader systems and structures of governance to ensure that a well-designed policy and legal environment achieves its full impact on employment in the MSE sector.

STATISTICAL AND METHODOLOGICAL ANNEX[1]

A.1 Statistical data by enterprise size classes: Sources, definitions and key indicators

A.1.1 Sources and definitions

The analysis of the employment situation and economic performance of MSEs is often hampered by the lack of statistical information disaggregated by enterprise size. For example, national account data in most countries refer to the whole economy; the specific contribution of MSEs, if captured at all, is not calculated. Despite this scarcity of data, especially in developing countries, various sources can be used. In general terms, two broad types of data sources can be distinguished according to whether they refer to economic units (enterprises or establishments) or households.

Data for analysis by enterprise size are often scarce

Establishment-level sources (establishment surveys, economic censuses or administrative registers) have the advantage of having reasonably accurate information on the size of the economic unit.[2] Moreover, employment data can be combined with other data on the enterprises' economic performance. The downside is that coverage is incomplete, especially with regard to the smallest and the unregistered enterprises. Establishment-level sources are often restricted to the manufacturing sector and include little information on the characteristics of individual workers, such as education, wages and employment quality.

---

[1] This Annex draws heavily on Christensen and Goedhuys (forthcoming) and on contributions from Christine Enzler and Micheline Goedhuys.

[2] In general, available employment data from sources of this type relate to establishments rather than enterprises. This introduces a distortion because some micro- or small establishments in fact belong to large enterprises and therefore should not be counted as "micro" or "small". This distortion may be avoided by excluding such small establishments belonging to large enterprises when the database includes a variable on the establishment status (i.e. independent establishment or establishment belonging to a larger enterprise). Data from administrative registers may underestimate employment levels, as some enterprises tend to declare a lower number of employees to avoid social security payments or other legal obligations.

Household-level sources (household surveys, labour force surveys, population censuses) cover own-account workers and workers in very small enterprises, as well as those working in larger enterprises. They also include non-manufacturing sectors. Good household-level sources often allow us to relate individual worker characteristics with information on income and employment quality. The disadvantage is that the information on the enterprise size will often be imprecise. Data gathering and data analysis need to be improved in many developing countries to expand the knowledge of the MSE sector.

The data presented here and in Chapter 2 on employment shares of MSEs are based on household-level sources, while data on the number of enterprises and the contribution to GDP are mainly based on establishment-level sources. In addition to compiling and tabulating information based on available statistical sources, this research project also included specific MSE surveys in each of the seven countries under studies (see section 2 of this annex).

There is no uniform definition for micro-, small and medium-sized enterprises worldwide

As mentioned in Chapter 1, there is no universally applied definition for micro- and small enterprises. Definitions vary enormously from one country to the next. Some countries even employ multiple definitions across different government agencies. The most commonly used definition criteria are employment, turnover and productive assets. In this book, we refer to enterprises with one to nine workers as micro-enterprises, and to enterprises with 10 to 49 workers as small enterprises. This includes self-employed workers, who were included in the analysis of employment data and policy assessment, but excluded from the MSE survey samples.

Table A.1 gives an overview of the statistical definitions used in the countries under study. These definitions are often different from the official definitions used for the purpose of policy design. Whenever possible, the statistical indicators in the next subsection are based on the generic definition to ensure comparability across countries.

A.1.2 Some key indicators to measure the contribution of MSEs

This subsection presents some statistical data that measure the contribution of MSEs to the economy and to employment in the seven countries under study, as well as in selected other countries for comparison. Specifically, these indicators relate to the share of MSEs in the total number of enterprises, to the contribution of MSEs to GDP, and to the employment share of MSEs in total non-agricultural employment.

MSEs account for 97 to 99 per cent of all enterprises

In virtually all countries, MSEs are a huge majority of enterprises. Among the countries under study, available data indicate that MSEs account for a share of between 97.5 per cent and 99.7 per cent of all enterprises (table A.2). These numbers may still

Table A.1 Definitions of enterprise size classes in the countries under study

Country	Source	Criteria for size classes	Micro	Small	Medium	Large	Notes on coverage
Chile	CASEN (Household survey)	Number of persons engaged	2–9 (excluding self-employed)	10–49	(Medium and large classed together) <50		The survey includes formal and informal enterprises in all sectors, but for the analysis agriculture has been excluded. Size classes exclude the army and workers not knowing the business size.
	Internal Revenue Sevice (SII) (and ENIA)	Annual turnover (in UF)	1–2,400	2,401–25,000	25,001+		
Guinea	"Programme cadre pour le soutien au développement du secteur privé, 1998"	Turnover (in millions of Guinean francs)	<15	(Small and medium classed together) 15–500		>500	
		Number of employees	1–3	3–60		>60	
		Investment (in millions of Guinean francs)	<10	10–300		>300	
		Type of management and organization	Manager is the owner, and organization is rudimentary	Managed by owner or a delegation, modest organizational structure		Managed by a delegation and very structured organization	
	"Code des Investissements, 1998"	Assets (excluding land used and li-quidities, millions Guinean francs)	(Implicitly: maximum 5 workers)	(Small and medium classed together) Value of assets: 15–500			Formal enterprises only.

Cont./

Table A.1 Definitions of enterprise size classes in the countries under study *Continued*

Country	Source	Criteria for size classes	Micro	Small	Medium	Large	Notes on coverage
Guinea *Cont./*		Number of permanent workers			>5		
		Bookkeeping			Regular bookkeeping		
	Kourouma (2003)	Number of permanent workers (including owner)	1–4	(Small and medium classed together) 5–49			
Peru	Country papers (using ENAHO data for urban Peru and Metropolitan Lima)	Number of workers (including owner)	1–9	10–49	50–199	200+	
Pakistan	Census of Establishment (1988)	Number of persons engaged	1–9	10–49	50–99	100+ (also available: large 100–199 and very large 200+)	Including government-owned establishments, formal and informal sector.
South Africa	National Small Business Act (1996) and Ntsika Enterprise Promotion Agency	Paid employees and formality	0–4 employees, or informal. For Ntsika, divided into "survivalist" (income lower than poverty line, no paid employees, asset value negligible), "micro" (informal with less than 5 paid employees), and "very small" (formal with 0–9 paid employees).	10–49 (sometimes include very small)	(Medium and large classed together) 50–99 (except for mining, electricity, manufacturing and construction)		

Country	Source	Criterion					Remarks
	Labour Force Survey	Number of regular workers (employees, employers and self-employed)	1-9	10-49	<50		
Tanzania, United Rep. of	Small and Medium Enterprise Development Policy: 2002-2012 (draft, Nov. 2001)	Number of employees	1-4	5-49	50-100	>101	Includes only national businesses registered and paying First Category taxes. Commerce and other less visible sectors might be unregistered, thus under-represented.
		Capital investment (in millions of Tanzanian shillings)	>5.0	5.1-200	200.1-800	>800	
		Turnover (in millions of Tanzanian shillings)	0-12.0	12-150	150-300	>300	
	Country papers	Number of employees	1-9	10-49	50-100	101+	
European Union	European Commission (2002)	Number of employees	0-9 (including self-employed and enterprises with only unpaid family workers)	10-49	50-249	250+	

Table A.2   Estimated share of MSEs, most recent year (percentage of total number of enterprises)

	Micro	Small	MSEs
Chile (1999)	83.5	14.0	97.5
Guinea (1995)[1]	96.0	..	..
Pakistan (1988)[2]	97.2	2.5	99.7
South Africa (2000)[3]	..	..	98.0
Viet Nam (1999)[4]	..	..	98.0
EU-19 (2000)[5]	93.1	5.9	99.0

Notes: .. not available. [1] Due to restricted data availability, data for Guinea refer to the share of informal enterprises in private non-agricultural enterprises. [2] Data for Pakistan only cover the non-agricultural sector. [3] Data for South Africa include medium-sized enterprises. [4] Data for Viet Nam refer to household enterprises, a large majority of them being micro-enterprises. [5] Europe-19 includes the European Union countries, Iceland, Liechtenstein, Norway and Switzerland.

Source: Country papers and European Commission (2002).

underestimate the share of MSEs, given that many of them are not registered with statistical offices and are thus not captured.

As mentioned in Chapter 2, most non-agricultural employment in the countries under study can be found in MSEs (table A.3).[3]

In order to analyse the creation of employment by MSEs (rather than just their overall share of total employment), it is necessary to use longitudinal data to assess the employment creation in existing enterprises over time as well as enterprise births and deaths. In Peru and the United Republic of Tanzania, where such longitudinal data sets exist, an analysis of employment flows in MSEs has been carried out (Chacaltana, 2001; Goedhuys, 2002; Tibandebage et al., 2003).

Unfortunately, in most countries under study, such data sets do not exist. In order to fill this data gap, the MSE surveys carried out in these countries (see following section) contain information enabling analysis of employment flows over the last two years in surveyed enterprises. However, these data do not allow comparison with medium-sized and large enterprises because the surveys were restricted to MSEs. The comparative analysis of employment growth in enterprises of different sizes therefore has often been limited to anecdotal evidence and estimates of the variation of the MSE employment share over time. As can be seen in table A.4, available data point to an increase of the employment share of MSEs in most countries in the 1990s. Unfortunately, several of the sources for the data presented in table A.3 were not consistent over time. For example, in Chile, the CASEN changed the question referring to

[3] For statistical data on informal sector and micro-enterprise employment in other countries, see Hussmanns and du Jeu (2002) and ILO (2002e) and, for Latin America, ILO (2002d).

Table A.3   Contribution of micro- and small enterprises to non-agricultural employment, most recent year (percentages)

	Micro	Small	MSEs[1]
Chile (2000)	44.7	7.7	62.4
Guinea (1994)[2]	82.4	..	..
Pakistan (1988)	59.0	15.0	74.0
Peru (2000)[3]	70.5	8.4	78.9
South Africa (2000)	45.5	23.6	69.1
Tanzania, United Rep. of (2000)[4]	54.9	..	..
Viet Nam (1999)[5]	..	..	65.0
Europe-19 (2000)[6]	34.3	19.0	53.2

Notes: .. not available. [1] MSEs include self-employed persons. Due to lack of data availability, informal sector employment has been used as a proxy for MSE employment in the United Republic of Tanzania and Guinea. [2] Urban informal sector employment as a share of non-agricultural employment. [3] Share of MSEs in urban employment. [4] Informal sector employment as a share of non-agricultural employment. [5] Share of private sector, which includes formal private enterprises and semi-informal household enterprises, in total employment. [6] Includes the European Union countries, Iceland, Liechtenstein, Norway and Switzerland, and refers to non-primary private employment.

Source: Country papers and European Commission (2002).

Table A.4   Changes in MSE share of non-agricultural employment in the 1990s in countries under study

	Beginning 1990s	End 1990s or most recent
Chile (1992, 2002)[1]	46.7	45.3
Guinea (1987, 1994)[2]	75.4	82.4
Pakistan (1988, 1997)[3]	17.0	26.3
Peru (1990, 2000)[4]	70.6	77.6
South Africa (1988, 1999)[5]	39.0	44.0
EU-19 (1995, 2000)[6]	51.2	53.2

Notes: Due to limited availability of data series, coverage of data differs for some countries from data presented in other tables. [1] Share of enterprises with fewer than ten workers in total non-agricultural employment. [2] Share of the informal sector employment in non-agricultural employment. [3] Contribution of manufacturing household and small establishments employing fewer than ten persons in total manufacturing employment, estimated from data in the Labour Force Surveys and the Surveys of Household and Manufacturing Industries. [4] Data refer to Lima only. [5] Formal small and medium enterprises in the manufacturing sector only. [6] Includes the European Union countries, Iceland, Liechtenstein, Norway and Switzerland, and refers to non-primary private employment.

Source: Country papers, except for Chile: Encuesta Nacional de Empleo and EU-19: European Commission (2002).

enterprise size between 1996 and 1998, making it necessary to use the Encuesta Nacional de Empleo, which only allows the measurement of the share of micro-enterprises. In Peru, data prior to 1996 only cover Lima.

Figure A.1 Estimated contribution of MSEs to GDP and employment (percentages)

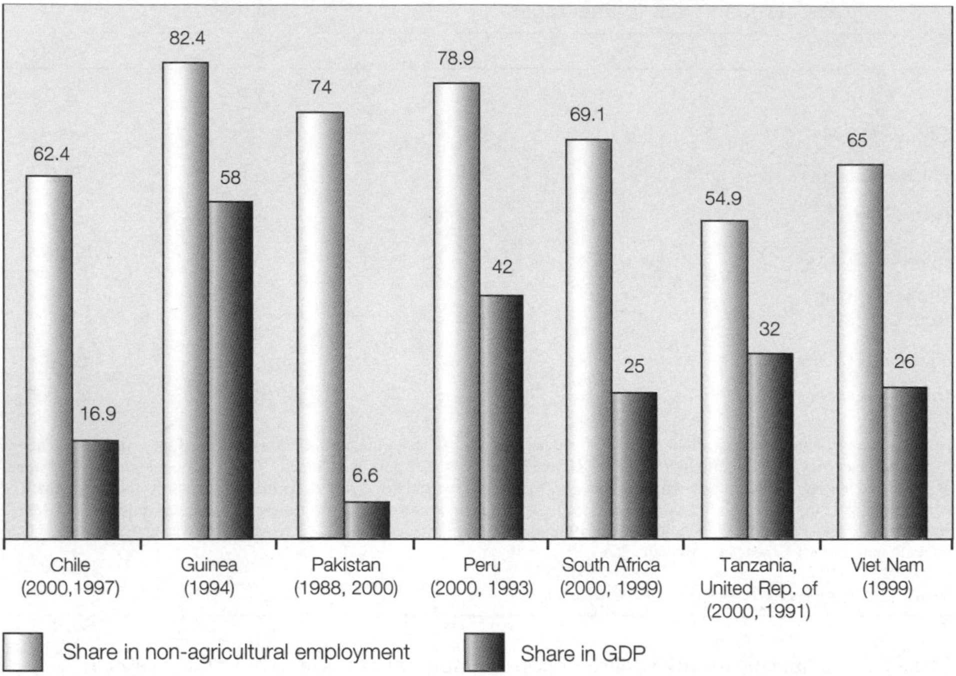

Share in non-agricultural employment   Share in GDP

Notes: Some studies have estimated the share of MSEs in GDP at a much higher level. Depending on the methodology, the size of enterprises covered and the varying results obtained in surveys, figures on GDP contribution of MSEs and the informal sector may be either under- or overestimated. For more information on the employment figures used in this graph, please see the notes to table A.3. Most GDP figures are estimates and should be used with caution. The GDP contributions refer to the following: Chile: contribution of MSEs to national sales (the source includes only enterprises paying taxes in the first category so smaller firms' contribution, in particular in less visible sectors such as commerce, is likely to be underestimated); Guinea: urban informal sector; Pakistan: SMEDA estimation of the MSMEs' contribution based on various sources, some of which probably not including enterprises with no permanent location; Peru: contribution to GNP; South Africa: formal sector only; United Republic of Tanzania: informal sector; Viet Nam: formal domestic private sector and non-farm household enterprises.

Sources: Country papers.

MSEs make a substantial contribution to GDP

Statistical information on the contribution of MSEs to GDP is often very difficult to obtain. This is because national accounts usually do not distinguish the economic contribution of enterprises by the size of the business. Moreover, in many countries, the contribution of MSEs that are not registered with all relevant government agencies may not be captured at all, thus implying an underestimation of total GDP figures.

Given this scarcity of statistical data, the estimates provided in figure A.1 should be understood as merely indicative. The methodologies used to obtain these estimates varied considerably across countries, leading to serious underestimations in a number of cases.

Given the relative scarcity of statistical information in many countries, the Job Creation in Small and Medium-Sized Enterprises Recommendation, 1998 (No. 189), suggests that member States should, with a view to the formulation of policies, collect national data on the MSE sector covering quantitative and qualitative aspects of employment. At the same time, data collection should not result in undue administrative burdens for small and medium-sized enterprises.

A.2 The ILO MSE Surveys 2001: Methodology, sample composition and analysis

A.2.1 Survey design and samples

As part of the comparative research project, ILO/SEED designed and commissioned MSE surveys in each of the seven countries under study. The surveys were designed to better understand how policy and legal environments influence the volume and quality of employment in MSEs. This section will outline the objectives, sample composition and some main results of these surveys.[4]

The surveys were based on a generic MSE survey questionnaire that was developed as part of the research project. The national consultants commissioned to carry out the survey in each country were provided with this generic questionnaire and a "survey kit" that deals with the adaptation of the generic questionnaire to national circumstances, as well as with the steps for the sample design and survey implementation. *Main topics covered by the surveys*

A first set of questions in the generic questionnaire captures the major characteristics of the enterprise, such as size, sector of activity, legal status, year of establishment, location, and some key entrepreneur characteristics, such as education, age, former work experience and gender. Related sets of questions assess the enterprise's position in input markets and output markets. On the input markets, the access of the enterprise to credit, business information and infrastructure is assessed. The degree of diversification and the size of the geographical market provide some information on the enterprise's position in output markets.

A subsequent set of questions identifies the major source of influence for employment and investment decisions. Some of these questions track employment decisions made by business owners and managers in the last two years. The respondent entrepreneur indicates to what extent his or her employment decisions and investment behaviour have been the direct or indirect result of one or more policies, laws or regulations, or whether they have been determined by conditions in input and output markets.

In each of the seven countries, a sample of approximately 300 MSEs was interviewed in 2001 (except in Peru, where the *Sampling strategy*

---

[4] The surveys are documented and analysed in more detail in Christensen and Goedhuys (forthcoming) and in the country reports.

sample was larger). In total, 2,730 enterprises were included in the survey. Each country sample consists of enterprises with fewer than 50 workers, including contributing family workers. To achieve a broad cross-sectional sample, the sample frames in each of the seven countries were drawn on the basis of four main control variables: (i) enterprise size, (ii) sex of the business owner, (iii) business sector (trade, services, manufacturing) and (iv) location, including rurally based enterprises and enterprises active in urban areas.[5] In particular, as the intent was not to gather representative data of the MSE sector but to ensure that researchers could examine gender questions, women-owned MSEs were purposely over-represented in the samples.[6]

The distribution of the enterprises over the different size classes and sectors was determined on the basis of national statistics, reports or censuses, where these exist. However, the lack of reliable or complete data regarding the numbers and importance of business sizes and sectors in the rural and urban areas, especially with regard to micro-enterprises, meant that the final sample was decided upon in collaboration with national consultants. These inevitable country-specific factors imply that the final samples (table A.5) cannot be considered "representative" of the MSE universe in the seven countries in a strict statistical sense.

- In Guinea, given the current knowledge of the MSE sector, it was decided that the sample would be evenly split between men and women and that it would include a 50 per cent share of micro-enterprises (up to four workers, in keeping with national definitions). However, in the comparative analysis in this book and in Christensen and Goedhuys (forthcoming), enterprises with two to nine workers have been classified as micro-enterprises to ensure consistency across countries.

- In Pakistan, after the sample drawing was completed, it was found that an insufficient number of women were available in some sectors. It was decided to carry out a booster sample of 25 women entrepreneurs, arriving at a sample size of 333 entrepreneurs in total. The final sample in Pakistan, however, still had a large majority of men.

- Peru was the only country where the MSE survey sample can be considered representative for urban micro- and small enterprises in Lima. The Peruvian survey was constructed via a two-step approach: first, a household survey was carried out to identify economic activity among the members of the sample households, then enterprises identified in the first step were surveyed. The

---

[5] Rural agricultural enterprises were excluded from the surveys.

[6] As the samples were not nationally representative and were limited to MSEs, the information on the MSE share in the economy and employment in Ch. 2 are drawn from national sources and not from the MSE surveys.

Table A.5   Composition of survey sample (percentages)

	Size class		Sector			Sex	Location	
	1–9 workers	10+ workers	Trade	Services	Manufac- turing	Female-run enterprises	Rural enterprises	Total no. of enterprises
Chile	53.7	46.3	37.0	36.0	27.0	35.0	16.0	300
Guinea	83.3	16.7	45.8	37.5	16.7	50.0	25.0	312
Pakistan	50.8	49.2	30.6	37.2	32.1	14.4	39.6	333
Peru	78.1	21.9	34.2	33.0	32.9	26.0	14.1	894
South Africa	89.2	10.8	35.1	30.8	34.1	40.5	14.0	279
Tanzania, United Rep. of	67.0	33.0	28.7	37.7	33.7	43.0	23.7	300
Viet Nam	63.8	36.2	40.1	30.4	29.5	30.4	37.2	312
Total no. of enterprises	1 937	793	970	938	822	878	610	2 730

Source: ILO MSE Surveys 2001.

sample also differs from those of the other countries under study, as the total sample size is larger (see table A.5).[7]

- In Viet Nam, unregistered enterprises were not included in the sample. Although semi-formal household enterprises are included as registered, this may introduce a bias because other enterprises, which are even more informal, are excluded.

Table A.5 presents the composition of the final sample for the seven countries, showing the percentage distribution in the different size classes and over the different sectors. The last column indicates the total number of enterprises interviewed in each country.

Sample composition

The majority of enterprises are micro-enterprises, with 1,937 enterprises or 71 per cent of the total sample employing fewer than 10 workers. The three economic sectors – trade, service and manufacturing – were quite evenly distributed in all countries except in Guinea, where the final sample allocation saw a much higher share of both trade and service enterprises compared to only 16 per cent of manufacturing enterprises. A rural/urban split was also strived for in the national sample compositions.

A.2.2 Measuring compliance with registration requirements

It is not easy to measure the compliance of MSEs with government regulations. Enterprises may be reluctant to report that they evade taxes, and comparison across countries has to take differences in

The challenge of measuring compliance

---

[7] In addition to the 894 sample enterprises with two to 49 workers, the sample also included 309 self-employed. These were excluded from the sample for the comparative analysis.

regulatory requirements into account. In this book, MSE survey responses regarding compliance with registration requirements have been used to analyse this topic. Obviously, registration does not cover all aspects of compliance. For example, an enterprise may be registered with tax authorities but still evade most of the taxes due. On the other hand, even enterprises that are not registered may be compelled to pay taxes.[8]

Comparing compliance across countries

We have developed some variables to endeavour to capture compliance across countries. As mentioned in Chapter 3, this analysis focuses on general business registrations. By this, we mean registrations that are required for an enterprises to operate legally, regardless of the economic sector. This thus excludes registration that is only required for enterprises in specific economic sectors or for specific purposes (such as exporting or participating in public tenders). For each country, the most important general registration requirements in the areas of business laws and regulations, taxation and labour have been identified, and are presented in table A.6.

Based on these registration requirements, several variables have been defined.[9] Finally, in order to synthesize the degree of compliance with registration requirements, a synthesis variable has been constructed (RegSYNTH). This variable considers all registration requirements included in the variables, as well as some other general registration requirements reported in coloured characters in table A.6. It takes the value 0 if an enterprise has none of the registrations under consideration, 1 if it has one or more, but not all registrations, and 2 if it has all of them. Moreover, the variable corrects for the fact that some enterprises are not required to register with labour authorities because they do not hire employees or their number remains below the minimum threshold under national legislation.[10]

The resulting synthesis information concerning compliance with registration requirements has been reported in table 3.2 in Chapter 3. Moreover, this information has also been used to analyse the link between compliance with registration requirements and access to formal credit in Chapter 4. Table A.7 reports the compliance with main registration requirements by sex of the business owner-manager. In all countries except Guinea, men-owned enterprises tend to have a higher degree of compliance with registration requirements than women-owned enterprises.

---

[8] For a summary, brief analysis and presentation of the survey results, see Ch. 3, pp. 49–73 and table 3.1.

[9] See notes to table A.6 for definitions.

[10] For example, an enterprise with two employees in the United Republic of Tanzania complies with all registration requirements even if it is not registered with the Employment Fund (PPF/NSSF), because this registration is only required for enterprises with four or more employees.

Table A.6   Simplified summary of basic registration requirements for MSEs

	Chile	Guinea	Pakistan	Peru	South Africa	Tanzania, United Rep. of	Viet Nam
Business regulations – national	Obtaining a registration number (Rol Unico Tributario, RUT)	Office de Promotion des Investissements Privés (OPIP)	–	–	–	–	Planning and Investment Services, provincial level (compulsory for enterprises according to the Enterprise Law)
Business regulations – local	Local permit	–	–	Municipio/ administración local	Local authority	Local authority (Municipal/District /City Council)	People's Committee, district level (compulsory for household enterprises)
Variable RegBR	RUT *and* Local permit	OPIP	Does not apply	Municipio/ administración local	Local authority	Local authority	Planning and Investment Services or People's Committee
Tax authorities	Iniciación de actividades (Initiation of activities)	Direction Nationale des Impôts (DNI)	Income Tax Department Sales Tax Department Excise Tax Department	Superintendencia de Administración Tributaria (SUNAT)	Receiver of Revenue	(Tanzania Revenue Authority) TRA	Enterprise Income Tax VAT Excise Tax/ Licence Tax Special Consumption Tax High Income Tax

Cont./

167

Table A.6 Simplified summary of basic registration requirements for MSEs *Continued*

	Chile	Guinea	Pakistan	Peru	South Africa	Tanzania, United Rep. of	Viet Nam
Variable RegTAX	Initiation of Activities	DNI	Income Tax Department	SUNAT	Receiver of Revenue	TRA	Enterprise Income tax
Labour authorities	No separate registration for the enterprise	Agence Guinéenne pour la promotion de l'Emploi (AGUIPE) Caisse nationale de sécurité sociale	Employees' Old Age Benefit Institution (EOBI) Employment Social Security Institution (ESSI) Directorate of Labour Welfare (DLW) (Registration with labour authorities compulsory for enterprises with 10 or more paid workers)	Ministerio de Trabajo y Promoción Social (MTPS) (compulsory for enterprises with paid workers) Entidad administradora del Seguro Social de Salud (EsSalud – antes IPSS) (compulsory for enterprises with paid workers) Oficina de Normalización Previsional/Administradora de Fondo de Pensiones	Unemployment Insurance Fund Workmen's Compensation Fund	Employment Fund (PPF/NSSF) (compulsory for all enterprises with 4 or more employees) Registration under the Factory Ordinance (1952) (compulsory but not in the data)	Job Creation Fund (optional)
Variable RegLAB	Does not apply	AGPE	DLW	MTPS	Unemployment Insurance Fund	PPF/NSSF	Does not apply

Authorities related to trade and industry			Export Promotion Bureau (EPB) (optional) Securities and Exchange Commission of Pakistan (SECP) (optional) Registrar of partnership	Ministerio del Sector (not included in the survey)	Department of Trade and Industry	Ministry of Trade and Industry (compulsory only for certain sectors)
Synthesis variable RegSYNTH	RUT Local permit Initiation of activities	OPIP DNI AGPE	Income Tax Department Sales Tax Department Excise Tax Department DLW EOBI ESSI	Municipio/administración local SUNAT MTPS EsSalud	Local authority Receiver of Revenue Unemployment Insurance Fund	Local authorities TRA Employment fund

Import–Export Tax (compulsory only for enterprises engaging in foreign trade)

Planning and Investment Services or People's Committee
Enterprise Income Tax
VAT
Excise Tax/Licence Tax
Special Consumption Tax
High-Income Tax

Note: General registration requirements included in the synthesis variable RegSYNTH are in colour. RegBR: This variable refers to business regulations at national and local level. The variable takes the value 1 if the enterprise complies with registration requirements in this field, and 0 if it does not. RegTAX: This variable refers to registration with business income tax authorities. The variable takes the value 1 if the enterprise is registered with tax authorities and 0 if it is not. The variable does not include other tax authorities in cases where registration with separate tax authorities is required. RegLAB: This variable refers to registration with general labour authorities. The variable takes the value 1 if the enterprise is registered with labour authorities and 0 if it is not.

Source: ILO/SEED based on country papers and ILO MSE Surveys 2001.

Table A.7   Compliance with main registration requirements by sex, 2001 (share in percentages)

		Not complying with any basic registration requirements	Complying with some, but not all, registration requirements	Complying with all basic registration requirements
Chile	Male	5.6	28.2	66.2
	Female	12.4	23.8	63.8
Guinea	Male	28.8	68.6	2.6
	Female	16.7	76.3	7.1
Pakistan	Male	31.2	61.8	7.0
	Female	62.5	37.5	0.0
Peru	Male	10.0	46.7	43.4
	Female	9.9	55.6	34.5
South Africa	Male	52.4	34.3	13.3
	Female	75.2	19.5	5.3
Tanzania,	Male	2.9	46.8	50.3
United Rep. of	Female	2.3	54.3	43.4
Viet Nam	Male	6.0	93.5	0.5
	Female	8.4	90.5	1.1

Note: In Viet Nam, enterprises not registered with any government agency have not been included in the sample.

Source: ILO MSE Surveys 2001.

A.2.3 Determinants of employment growth: A multivariate logit analysis

In order to find associations between key enterprise and entrepreneur characteristics on the one hand, and enterprise growth versus stagnation and contraction on the other hand, the sample MSEs are split into two groups. The first group includes 1,305 enterprises that have expanded employment during the period 1999 to 2001, equivalent to 48 per cent of the total sample across the seven countries. The remaining group of 1,425 enterprises have stagnated or reduced the number of workers over the same period.

To investigate the joint effect of various variables on employment growth, a logit analysis or logistic regression was carried out. Logit analysis is a technique with similarities to the multiple regression or Ordinary Least Squares (OLS) technique, but it is used when the dependent variable is dichotomous or binary. This is the case in our analysis, as the dependent variable is a binary variable equalling 1 if the enterprise has grown over the period 1999 to 2001, and 0 if the enterprise has stagnated or contracted. However, logit analysis has an estimation technique different to that of OLS. It compares the probability that an event occurs to the probability that it does not occur, or, in our particular case, it compares the probability that an enterprise has grown in terms of employment to the probability that it has not grown.[11] The use of this technique does not change in any manner the interpretation of the sign of the estimated coefficient. A positive coefficient increases the probability, while a negative value reduces the predicted probability.

We use the logistic regression technique to estimate the probability that enterprises have grown. Explanatory variables include enterprise age in logarithmic terms, enterprise size in 1999, location, sector of activity, formal status and geographical market. Table A.8 summarizes the estimation results and presents merely the estimated coefficients and their significance level.[12] The first column (All) refers to the estimation for the entire sample, with country dummy variables, the reference country being Peru. Pakistan is excluded from all estimations in this section because of missing values. The second until the seventh column are estimations for the countries separately. As the sample sizes for the separate country estimations are smaller, the number of explanatory variables may change.

Analysing the probability that an enterprise creates employment

From the first column, it is clear that for the entire sample, enterprise size and enterprise age are negatively related to the probability that enterprises have grown over the period 1999 to 2001. The effect is significant and holds when the estimations are made for the different countries separately. The negative enterprise age–growth relationship is in line with theoretical models of learning. Most previous studies also find a significant negative relationship between enterprise growth and enterprise size.[13] It should be noted, however, that Viet Nam seems to be an exception to this robust finding. In Viet Nam, initial enterprise size has a positive effect on the probability that the enterprises have grown in terms of employment.

Smaller enterprises are more likely to grow

Rural enterprises seem to have faced more growth constraints than enterprises in urban areas, the reference group of enterprises. The coefficient is negative and significant for the sample taken as a whole, as well as for Peru, the United Republic of Tanzania and Viet Nam. Sectoral differences are also observed. Enterprises in services and manufacturing have apparently been more successful in creating employment than trading businesses.

The estimations were also calculated to include four variables that capture entrepreneur characteristics (Christensen and Goedhuys, forthcoming). It was found that the sex of the entrepreneurs did not have a significant impact in any of the countries. For the entire sample, the youngest entrepreneurs (under 25 years old) were less

---

[11] Prob (event) / prob (no event) = $e^{a_0 + a_1 x_1 + \cdots + a_n x_n}$

[12] Christensen and Goedhuys (forthcoming) present the full estimation results, including measures of the goodness of fit of the estimated models.

[13] See Christensen and Goedhuys (forthcoming) for references to previous studies.

Table A.8   Estimation results for the logit analysis

	All	Chile	Guinea	Peru	South Africa	Tanzania, United Rep. of	Viet Nam
Constant	1.76***	−1.83***	0.07	2.64***	0.57	0.87	−1.06*
Log (enterprise age)	−0.16**	−0.22	−0.01	−0.31**	0.11	−0.00	−0.16
Log (size 1999)	−0.90***	−0.24*	−0.84***	−1.84***	−1.51***	−0.55***	0.47***
Rural	−0.32**	0.27	0.01	−0.52*	0.08	−0.85***	−0.66**
Services	0.37***	0.53	0.44	0.88***	0.76**	−0.02	−0.16
Manufacturing	0.14	0.72**	0.07	−0.13	0.94***	0.10	0.10
Formal	0.30**	1.03*	−0.01	0.86**	1.05***	−0.53	−0.27
National	0.62***	0.60*	1.07***	0.73***	..	0.05	0.39
Exporting	0.82***	0.61	1.86**	1.70**	..	0.76	0.37
Chile	−1.78***						
Guinea	−1.23***						
South Africa	−1.05***						
Tanzania, United Rep. of	−1.56***						
Viet Nam	−2.90***						

Note: .. not available; *** significant at the 1 per cent level; ** significant at the 5 per cent level; * significant at the 10 per cent level; values with no asterisk are not significant.

Source: Christensen and Goedhuys (forthcoming) based on the ILO MSE Surveys 2001.

Compliance is associated with a higher probability of growing

successful than older entrepreneurs in making their enterprises grow. The achievement of higher levels of formal education (an academic degree) is significantly positive for employment creation in Peru and South Africa. No significant impact was found for lower levels of formal education.

Enterprises registered with business licence or tax authorities have faced better growth opportunities in Chile, Peru, and South Africa. Measured at the sample means and considering the variables included in the logit estimations, the formal status raises the probability of enterprise growth from 70 per cent to 85 per cent in Peru, from 12 per cent to 28 per cent in Chile and from 33 per cent to 59 per cent in South Africa. In none of the countries under study has a statistically significant negative correlation between registration and employment growth been found.

As mentioned in Chapter 3, these results are in line with other studies, which find that formality is related to superior growth. According to these studies, formality captures legitimacy and reputation of enterprises in the industry. Registration provides enterprises with an institutional standing in the eyes of law-enforcing agencies, consumers, suppliers, police officers and other key actors, and facilitates contractual relationships with clients, suppliers and third parties. Formal enterprises can also gain better

Box A.1   Correlation between employment growth and different registration variables

In order to test the correlation between employment growth and compliance with regulations, five logit analyses with different registration variables have been carried out.

The summary table below shows the coefficients of different registration variables in a logit estimation with the following additional explanatory variables: the size in 1999, the enterprise age in 2001, location (urban/rural) and the economic sector (manufacturing, services, commerce).

The first four logit estimations each have one explanatory variable, capturing the effect of registration/legitimacy effects on growth. RegBR measures the effect of registering the business; it is mostly positive, except for Viet Nam and Chile where the coefficient is not significant. RegTAX measures the effect of registering with tax authorities.

In the last logit estimation, there are two explanatory variables. RegBR captures the effect of having a business registration on growth. Adding Formal2 to the same logit allows us to measure the additional effect of also being registered with tax authorities, given that the enterprise already has a business registration. It is therefore not surprising that the sign turns negative in many cases. The legitimacy effect is already captured in the RegBR variable.

In general, it seems that business registration has the most positive effect on growth, which is quite logical as it involves reputation effects for the enterprise, and is in line with the idea that legitimacy becomes an important resource allocation mechanism when market forces are not working properly. Registration with tax authorities can also grant legitimacy, but it involves a cost in the form of tax payments. In countries where taxation is high, this cost can outweigh the benefits (Guinea, the United Republic of Tanzania, Viet Nam) and the impact on growth can vary from one country to another.

The most robust findings are for Peru, Guinea, South Africa and Viet Nam. In Peru, a positive effect of legitimacy is derived from registering the business, and also from registering with tax authorities, albeit to a lesser extent (as explained above). From the last logit estimation it is clear that both forms of registration share the legitimacy effect, as both coefficients are positive. A lack of significance is not a point to focus on in this logit estimation (multicollinearity may be the reason). The same applies to South Africa.

In Guinea, it is clear that taxation is outweighing the benefits of legitimacy from registration with tax authorities; the positive impact comes from registering the business. A similar effect is at play in Viet Nam. For the United Republic of Tanzania, there are no significant findings, yet the results are not illogical. For Chile, the findings are more difficult to interpret.

Summary table: Logit estimations showing the correlation with employment growth
for different registration variables

	Total sample	Chile	Guinea	Peru	South Africa	Tanzania, United Rep. of	Viet Nam
RegBR	0.36***	−0.29	0.73**	0.89***	1.03***	0.23	−0.34
RegTAX	0.18	0.86*	−0.25	0.80**	0.99**	−0.03	−0.47*
Formal†	0.37***	1.0*	0.04	0.94***	1.04***	−0.49	−0.19
Formal2†	0.24**	−0.31	0.45	0.82***	1.12***	0.16	−0.59**
RegBR ††	0.41**	0.16	2.11**	0.57	0.69	0.16	0.06
Formal2	−0.05	−0.47	−1.57	0.33	0.52	0.12	−0.62*

Notes: † Formal=1 if RegBR=1 *or* RegTAX=1; Formal2=1 if RegBR=1 *and* RegTAX=1; †† one logit estimation with both RegBR and Formal2 as explanatory variables. For levels of significance, see note to table A.8.

Source: Calculations provided by Micheline Goedhuys, based on data from the ILO MSE Surveys 2001.

access to scarce resources. Therefore, formal status may grant legitimacy and open up additional growth opportunities.

However, the analysis of the reasons that MSE owner-managers give for not registering, as well as the mapping of registration requirements in the country papers, suggest that the process of registering can be costly. The cost can be so high that some MSEs are not in a position to meet it. In some cases, the mere collection of information about registration, the registration process itself and the subsequent taxation and fulfilment of regulations impose a barrier to entry into the formal economy, and thus hamper the smooth transition of micro-enterprises toward a larger size.

The positive correlation between compliance and employment growth is fairly robust to the use of different registration variables, although the correlation is more positive for business registration than for tax registration (box A.1).

Access to export markets increases the likelihood of growing

Finally, the size of the output market also seems to be strongly related to enterprise growth. Compared to the reference group of enterprises which produce for local markets, enterprises serving the national market have been significantly more likely to grow, and the likelihood of growing is even higher for exporting enterprises, as the coefficients of "national" and "exporting" indicate.

BIBLIOGRAPHY

Abuodha, C.; Bowles, R. 2000a. "Business licence reform in Kenya and its impact on small enterprises", in *Small Enterprise Development*, Vol. 11, No. 3, pp. 16–24.

——; ——. 2000b. *Business licensing, compliance costs and deregulation in developing countries* (Hamburg, University of Hamburg).

Albu, M.; Scott, A. 2001. *Understanding livelihoods that involve micro-enterprise: Markets and technological capabilities in the SL framework* (Bourton, Warwickshire, Intermediate Technology Development Group).

Aliber, M. 2002. *South African microinsurance case study: Final report*, unpublished SFU/SEED Working Paper (Geneva, ILO).

Arroyo, J.; Nebelung, M. (eds.). 2002. *La micro y pequeña empresa en América Central. Realidad, mitos y retos* (San José/Guatemala, GTZ/ILO).

Bagachwa, M. 1996. *Macro policy framework for small-scale industries (SSI) in Africa: A Tanzanian case study*, paper presented at the ILO Tripartite policy seminar on Macroeconomic Policy Framework for Small-Scale Industries Development in Africa and Asia, 25–29 Mar., Nairobi, ILO.

Balkenhol, B.; Schütte, H. 2001. *Collateral, collateral law and collateral substitutes*, Social Finance Programme, Working Paper No. 26 (2nd edition) (Geneva, ILO).

Berry, A. 1995. *Creating an enabling policy environment for promotion of small enterprises: Traditional and innovative approaches*, Focal/CIS Discussion Papers, FC1995-10 (Toronto, Center for International Studies).

——. 1997. "Small-scale non-agricultural exports as a route to employment creation and poverty alleviation", in *Konjunkturpolitik*, Vol. 43, No. 3, pp. 275–298.

——; Mazumdar, D. 1991. "Small-scale industry in the Asian-Pacific Region", in *Asian-Pacific Economic Literature*, Vol. 5, No. 2, pp. 35–67.

Bertrand, M.; Kramarz, F. 2001. *Does entry regulation hinder job creation? Evidence from the French retail industry*, Working Paper 8211 (Cambridge, MA, National Bureau of Economic Research).

Chacaltana, J. 2001. *Políticas públicas y empleo en las pequeñas y microempresas en el Perú* (Lima, ILO).

Chandra, V., et. al. 2001a. *Constraints to growth and employment in South Africa. Report No. 1: Statistics from the large manufacturing firm survey* (Washington, DC, World Bank).

——. 2001b. *Constraints to growth and employment in South Africa. Report No. 2: Evidence from the small, medium and micro enterprise firm survey* (Washington, DC, World Bank).

Charmes, J. 1999. *Gender and informal sector: Contribution to* The World's Women 2000: Trends and Statistics (New York, United Nations).

Chen, M., et al. 2002. *Supporting workers in the informal economy: A policy framework*, Working Paper on the Informal Economy No. 2 (Geneva, ILO).

Chijoriga, M., et al. 2002. *The influence of national policies, laws and regulations on employment in micro and small enterprises*, SEED background paper (Geneva, ILO).

Christensen, J.; Goedhuys, M. Forthcoming. *Impact of national policy and legal environments on employment growth and investment in micro and small enterprises*, SEED Working Paper (Geneva, ILO).

Churchill, C., et al. 2002. *Making micro-insurance work for MFIs*, SFU/SEED Paper (Geneva, ILO).

Committee of Donor Agencies for Small Enterprise Development. 1995. *Small and micro-enterprise finance: Guiding principles for selecting and supporting intermediaries* (Washington, DC).

——. 1997. *Business Development Services for SMEs: Preliminary guideline for donor-funded interventions* (Washington, DC).

——. 2001. *Business development services for small enterprises: Guiding principles for donor intervention* (Washington, DC).

Cook, P.; Nixson. F. 2000. *Finance and small and medium-sized enterprise development*, Finance and Development Research Programme Paper No. 14 (Manchester, Institute for Development Policy and Management).

de Soto, H. 1989. *The other path. The invisible revolution in the Third World* (New York, Harper & Row).

——. 2000. *The mystery of capital: Why capitalism triumphs in the West and fails everywhere else* (New York, Basic Books).

Department of Trade and Industry, South Africa. 2000. *Summary report on "Examination of costs and interest rates in the small loans sector"* (Pretoria).

Dirección del Trabajo, Chile. 2000a. *Crónicas laborales*, No. 2, 1999 (Santiago).

——. 2000b. *Temas laborales*, Vol. 5, No. 14 (Santiago).

Djankov, S., et al. 2000. *The regulation of entry*, Discussion Paper 1904 (Cambridge, MA, Harvard Institute of Economic Research).

Durban City Council. 2000. *Durban's informal economy policy, prepared by the Technical Task Team and approved and adopted by the Joint Executive Committee – North and South Central Local Councils* (Durban).

English, E.P.; Hénault, G. (eds.). 1995. *Agents of change. Studies on the policy environment for small enterprise in Africa* (London, Intermediate Technology Publications).

Espinosa, M. 2001. *Informe final encuesta a micro y pequeñas empresas (SEED): El caso de Chile*, unpublished SEED background paper (Santiago, ILO).

——, et al. 2000. *Encuesta laboral ENCLA 1999. Informe de resultados* (Santiago, Dirección del Trabajo).

European Commission. 2002. *Observatory of European SMEs 2002/No.2. SMEs in Europe, including a first glance at EU candidate countries* (Luxembourg).

Flores, C. Forthcoming. *Creating a conducive policy environment for employment creation in MSEs in Chile*, SEED Working Paper (Geneva, ILO).

Franz, J.; Oesterdiekhoff, P. (eds.). 1998. *SME policies and policy formulation in SADC countries* (Gaborone, Friedrich Ebert Stiftung).

Gallup/BRB Pakistan. 2003. *The influence of the policy and legal environment on micro and small enterprises in Pakistan. A survey of 333 micro and small enterprises*, SEED Working Paper (Geneva, ILO).

Ginneken, W. van. 2003. *Extending social security: Policies for developing countries*, ESS Paper No. 13 (Geneva, ILO).

Goedhuys, M. 2002. *Employment creation and employment quality in African manufacturing firms*, SEED Working Paper No. 26 (Geneva, ILO).

——; Sleuwaegen, L. 1999. "Barriers to growth of firms in developing countries: Evidence from Burundi", in D. Audretsch and A.R. Thurik (eds.): *Innovation, industry evolution, and employment* (Cambridge, Cambridge University Press), pp. 297–314.

Gross, D.M. 2001. *Financial intermediation: A contributing factor to economic growth and employment*, Social Finance Programme Working Paper No. 27 (Geneva, ILO).

Gross, R. 2000. "Case study Namibia: Networking in the context of small enterprise promotion", in W. Zehender (ed.): *Networking with partners* (Eschborn, Deutsche Gesellschaft für Technische Zusammenarbeit), pp. 89–98.

Gumede, V. 2000. *Growth and exporting of small enterprises in South Africa. Some thoughts on policy and scope for further research*, 2000 Annual Forum, Trade and Industrial Policy Secretariat, Muldersdrift.

Haggblade, S., et al. 1990. "The effect of policy and policy reforms on non-agricultural enterprises and employment in developing countries", in F. Stewart, H. Thomas and T. de Wilde (eds.): *The other policy. The influence of policies on technology choice and small enterprise development* (London/Washington, IT Publications/Appropriate Technology International), pp. 58–98.

Held, G. 1999. *Políticas de crédito para empresas de menor tamaño con bancos de segundo piso: Experiencias recientes en Chile, Colombia y Costa Rica*. Serie Financiamiento del Desarollo, No. 84 (Santiago, ECLAC).

Hughes, A. 1999. *On enlarging employment by promoting small enterprises. A report for the United Nations Symposium on States, Markets and Social Progress: Roles and Co-operation of Public and Private Sector* (Beijing).

Hussmanns, R.; du Jeu, B. 2002. *ILO Compendium of official statistics on employment in the informal sector*, STAT Working Paper No. 2002–1 (Geneva, ILO).

International Labour Organization (ILO). 1996. *Macroeconomic policy and small-scale industry: Lessons from Asia and Africa* (New Delhi).

——. *Panorama Laboral '97* (Lima).

——. 1998. *Participatory cooperative policy making. A manual* (Geneva).

——. 1999a. *Panorama Laboral '99* (Lima).

——. 1999b. *Decent work*, Report of the Director-General, International Labour Conference, 87th Session, 1999 (Geneva)

——. 2000a. *Termination of employment digest* (Geneva).

——. 2000b. *World Labour Report 2000. Income security and social protection in a changing world.* (Geneva).

——. 2001a. *Panorama Laboral 2001* (Lima).

——. 2001b. *Social security. A new consensus* (Geneva).

——. 2002a. "Conclusions concerning decent work and the informal economy", in *Report of the Committee on the Informal Economy*, Provisional Record 25, International Labour Conference, 90th Session, 2002 (Geneva).

——. 2002b. *Decent work and the informal economy*, Report VI, International Labour Conference, 90th Session, 2002 (Geneva).

——. 2002c. *Global Employment Agenda: Discussion paper*, March (Geneva).

——. 2002d. *Panorama Laboral 2002* (Lima).

——. 2002e. *Women and men in the informal economy. A statistical picture* (Geneva).

Inter-American Development Bank. 2001. *Women's entrepreneurship in Latin America: An exploration of current knowledge* (Washington, DC).

——. 2002. *Acceso de las pequeñas y medianas empresas al financiamiento. Informe de trabajo* (Washington, DC).

Inversiones y Gestión Ltda. 2002. *Caracterización de las micro y pequeñas empresas. Versión preliminar* (Santiago, Comité de Fomento de la Micro y Pequeña Empresa).

Jansson, T. 2000. "Soportando el acoso de las formalidades. Registrar una empresa en América Latina", in *Microempresa. Informe de Avances*, Vol. 3, No. 1, pp. 1–5.

Jenkins, M. 1993. "Extending social security protection to the entire population: Problems and issues", in *International Social Security Review*, Vol. 46, No. 2, pp. 3–20.

Klein, E.; Tokman, V. (eds.). 1996. *Regulation and the informal economy: Microenterprises in Chile, Ecuador, and Jamaica* (Boulder, CO/London, Lynne Rienner).

Kourouma, M. 2001. *Examen empirique des facteurs déterminants du développement des micro et petites entreprises et de la stimulation des emplois en Guinée*, SEED background paper (Geneva, ILO).

——. 2003. *Promouvoir un environnement de développement des micro et petites entreprises guinéennes favorable à la création d'emplois décents*, SEED Working Paper No. 54 (Geneva).

Kuchta-Helbing, C. 2000. *Barriers to participation: The informal sector in emerging democracies*, Background Paper, Centre for International Private Enterprise (Washington, DC, CIPE).

Kwon, S. 2002. *Achieving health insurance for all: Lessons from the Republic of Korea*, ESS Paper No.1 (Geneva, ILO).

Levenson, A.; Maloney, W. 1998. *The informal sector, firm dynamics and institutional participation* (Washington, DC, World Bank).

Levi, M. 1997. "A model, a method, and a map: Rational choice in comparative and historical analysis", in M.I. Lichbach and A.S. Zuckerman (eds.): *Comparative politics: Rationality, culture and structure* (Cambridge, Cambridge University Press), pp. 19–41.

Maldonado, C., et al. 1999. *Le secteur informel en Afrique face aux contraintes légales et institutionelles* (Geneva, ILO).

McCormick, D., et al. 2001. *Enhancing institutional capacity for policy development, dialogue and advocacy: Role of associations and other community based organisations* (Nairobi, Institute for Development Studies, University of Nairobi).

Mead, D. 1994. "The contribution of small enterprises to employment growth in Southern and Eastern Africa", in *World Development*, Vol. 22, No. 12, pp. 1881–1894.

—; Liedholm. C. 1998. "The dynamics of micro and small enterprises in developing countries", in *World Development*, Vol. 26, No. 1, pp. 61–74.

Meier, R.; Pilgrim, M. 1994. "Policy-induced constraints on small enterprise development in Asian developing countries", in *Small Enterprise Development*, Vol. 5, No. 2, pp. 32–38.

Ministerio de Trabajo y Promoción Social. 2001. *Encuesta de micro y pequeña empresa (Informe de avance)*, unpublished SEED background paper (Geneva, ILO).

Mollentz, J. 2002. *Creating a conducive policy environment for employment creation in SMMEs in South Africa*, SEED Working Paper No. 35 (Geneva, ILO).

Morrisson, C., et al. 1994. *Micro-enterprises and the institutional framework in developing countries* (Paris, OECD Development Centre).

National Bureau of Statistics Tanzania. 2002. *Household Budget Survey 2000/01* (Dar es Salaam).

—. 2003. *Integrated Labour Force Survey, 2000/01 – Analytical report* (Dar es Salaam).

North, D. 1989. *Institutions, institutional change and economic performance* (Cambridge, Cambridge University Press).

—. 1994. *Institutions matter*, Economic History No. 9411004, Economics Working Paper Archive at WUTL (St. Louis, MO, Washington University).

Ntsika. 1998. *Basic Conditions of Employment Act – Impact assessment. Final report* (Pretoria).

—. 1999. *National small business regulatory review: Final report* (Pretoria).

Oi, W.; Idson, T. 1999. "Firm size and wages", in O. Ashenfelter and D. Card (eds.): *Handbook of labor economics*, Volume 3B (Amsterdam, Elsevier), pp. 2165–2212.

Onyango, I.; Tomecko, J. 1995. "Formulating a national policy for small enterprise: The Kenyan experience", in English and Hénault (eds.), pp. 25-44.

Organisation for Economic Co-operation and Development (OECD). 1996. *SMEs: Employment, innovation and growth: The Washington Workshop* (Paris).

—. 1999. *Regulatory reform for smaller firms* (Paris).

—. 2001. *Businesses' views on red tape: Administrative and regulatory burdens on small and medium-sized enterprises* (Paris).

Orlando, M.B.; Pollack, M. 2000. *Microenterprises and poverty. Evidence from Latin America* (Washington, DC, Inter-American Development Bank).

Osmani, S.R. 1995. *Macroeconomic policy and small scale industry in developing Asia*, SAAT Working Papers (New Delhi, ILO).

Pham, T.T.H. 2002. *Creating a conducive environment for employment creation in small enterprises in Viet Nam*, SEED Working Paper No. 31 (Geneva, ILO).

—; Nguyen, T.H.; Tran, C.D. 2002. *Survey on micro and small enterprises in Viet Nam. Survey report*, unpublished SEED background paper (Geneva/Hanoi, ILO/Viet Nam Chamber of Commerce and Industry).

Pharaoh, R.; Burton, P. 2001. *Evaluation of the International Labour Organisation's* Start and Improve Your Business *Programme in South Africa*, SEED background paper (Geneva, ILO).

Reinecke, G. 2000. *Inside the model: Politics, enterprise strategies and employment quality in Chile*, Ph.D. thesis (Hamburg, University of Hamburg).

—. 2002. *Small enterprises, big challenges: A literature review on the impact of the policy environment on the creation and improvement of jobs within small enterprises*, SEED Working Paper No. 23 (Geneva, ILO).

Rice, R. 2000. *Small enterprises as an essential part of the Indonesian development strategy* (Jakarta, USAID).

Robles, M., et al. 2001. *Estrategias y racionalidad de la pequeña empresa* (Lima, ILO).

Sartori, G. 1994. "Compare why and how: Comparing, miscomparing and the comparative method", in M. Dogan and A. Kazancigil (eds.): *Comparing nations: Concepts, strategies, substance* (Oxford, Basil Blackwell Ltd.), pp. 14–34.

Schaffner, J.A. 1998. "Premiums to employment in larger establishments: Evidence from Peru", in *Journal of Development Economics*, Vol. 55, No. 1, pp. 81–113.

Schlyter, C. 2002. *International labour standards and the informal sector: Developments and dilemmas*, Working Paper on the Informal Economy No. 3 (Geneva, ILO).

Schramm, B. 2002. *Sozialpolitik in Thailand. Die Entwicklung eines Wohlfahrtsstaates zwischen Paternalismus und Moderne* (Hamburg, Institut für Asienkunde).

Small and Medium-Sized Enterprise Development Authority (SMEDA). 2002. *Creating a conducive policy environment for micro, small and medium-sized enterprises in Pakistan*, SEED Working Paper No. 29 (Geneva, ILO).

Snodgrass, D.; Biggs, T. 1996. *Industrialization and the small firm. Patterns and policies* (San Francisco, International Center for Economic Growth/Harvard Institute for International Development).

Söderbom, M.; Teal, F. 2001. *Firm size and human capital as determinants of productivity and earnings*, Working Paper Series WPS/2001-9 (Oxford, Centre for the Study of African Economies).

Steel, W.; Takagi, Y. 1983. "Small enterprise development and the employment–output trade-off", in *Oxford Economic Papers*, Vol. 35, No. 3, pp. 423–446.

Stewart, F., et al. (eds.). 1990. *The other policy: The influence of policies on technology choice and small enterprise development* (London/ Washington, DC, IT Publications/Appropriate Technology International).

Tanburn, J., et al. 2001. *Business development services for small enterprises: Guiding principles for donor intervention* (Washington, DC, Committee of Donors for Small Enterprise Development).

Tendler, J. 2002. *Small firms, the informal sector, and the devil's deal* (Cambridge, MA, MIT).

Thomas, J. J. 1992. *Informal economic activity* (London, Harvester Wheatsheaf).

Tibandebage, P., et al. 2003. *Creating a conducive policy environment for employment creation in micro- and small enterprises in Tanzania*, SEED Working Paper No. 55 (Geneva, ILO).

Tokman, V., et al. 2001. *De la informalidad a la modernidad* (Santiago, ILO).

United Kingdom Department for International Development (DFID). 2000. *Making markets work better for the poor: A framework paper.* Prepared by the Economic Policy and Research Department together with the Business Partnership Department (London).

United Nations Development Programme (UNDP). 2002. *Human Development Report 2002* (New York).

Vega, M.L. 1996. "El derecho del trabajo y la pequeña empresa en América Latina: Resurge el debate", in *Asesoría Laboral*, Vol. 6, No. 64, pp. 8–15.

Verba, S. 1967. "Some dilemmas in comparative research", in *World Politics*, Vol. 20, No. 1, pp. 112–127.

von Potobsky, G. 1992. "Small and medium-sized enterprises and labour law", in *International Labour Review*, Vol. 131, No. 4, pp. 601–628.

White, S.; Chacaltana, J. 2002. *Enabling small enterprise development through a better business environment: Donor experiences in supporting reforms in the business environment* (Washington, DC, Committee of Donor Agencies for Small Enterprise Development, Working Group on Enabling Environment).

World Bank. 2001. "World business environment survey", in Transparency International (ed.): *Global Corruption Report 2001* (Berlin), pp. 249–251.

——. 2002. "Building institutions for markets", in *World Development Report 2002* (Washington, DC).

Xtenina, O. 2000. *Estimation of policy-induced factor price differences between small and large enterprises*, unpublished SEED background paper (Geneva, ILO).

INDEX

Note: Page numbers in **bold** refer to major text sections, those in *italic* to tables, figures and boxes. A subscript number appended to a page number indicates a page footnote, while a subscript 'n' indicates a footnote to a table, figure or box.

A PROGRAMME FOR SMALL ENTERPRISE TRAINING

START AND IMPROVE YOUR BUSINESS (SIYB)

Here is a system of interrelated training packages and support materials for small-scale entrepreneurs with limited previous exposure to management training. Start and Improve Your Business (SIYB) is part of the ILO's InFocus Programme on boosting employment through Small EnterprisE Development (ILO/SEED). IFP/SEED strives to assist member countries in their efforts to meet the employment challenge by creating sustainable quality jobs in the small-scale private enterprise sector.

SIYB projects worldwide work closely with government ministries, employers' organizations, workers' organizations, NGOs and the private sector. For more information on the programme, contact:

International Labour Office
InFocus Programme on boosting employment through Small EnterprisE Development
(ILO/SEED)
CH-1211 Geneva 22
Switzerland
Fax no. 41 22 799 7978
E-mail: ifpseed@ilo.org
Website : http:/www.ilo.org/seed

START YOUR BUSINESS

International Edition
ILO, 2003

Handbook	30 Swiss francs	ISBN 92-2-111635-2
Workbook	30 Swiss francs	ISBN 92-2-111636-0
Business Plan	10 Swiss francs	ISBN 92-2-111637-9

Start Your Business provides guidance, information and exercises to help you start a small business of your own.

— assess your potential as an entrepreneur

— develop your business idea

— assess your market

— develop a marketing plan

— organize your business

— cost your products or services

— estimate your start-up capital

— make financial plans

— understand business responsibilities

— choose a legal form for your business

— complete a Business Plan for your business

A PROGRAMME FOR SMALL ENTERPRISE TRAINING

IMPROVE YOUR BUSINESS

International Edition
ILO, 1999

Basics	30 Swiss francs	ISBN 92-2-110853-8
Trainer's Guide	10 Swiss francs	ISBN 92-2-110864-3

Improve Your Business Basics is designed to build upon the knowledge and skills learnt through the Start Your Business programme. There are six topics in Improve Your Business Basics:

— Marketing

— Buying

— Stock control

— Costing

— Record keeping

— Financial planning

Also available in French.

A PROGRAMME FOR SMALL ENTERPRISE TRAINING

START AND IMPROVE YOUR BUSINESS: THE GAME

International Edition
ILO, to be published in 2004

Price to be announced   ISBN 92-2-110089-8

The SIYB Game is a major training tool of the SIYB programme. It is a simulation that complements the SIYB training of potential and existing entrepreneurs, assisting participants to understand the realities of starting and operating a successful business.

Using a modular approach, it provides a practical experience of running a business inside the four walls of a training room. It is designed to give seminar participants an opportunity to make the kinds of decisions – and deal with the consequences of those decisions – which they must make in the real business world.

A Facilitator's Manual is included in the SIYB Game package.